The Challenge of Rock and Mountain Climbing

The Challenge of
Rock and Mountain Climbing

Ruth & John Mendenhall

Illustrated
by
Valerie P. Cohen

STACKPOLE BOOKS

Published by
STACKPOLE BOOKS
Cameron and Kelker Streets
P. O. Box 1831
Harrisburg, PA 17105

First edition, May 1969
Second edition, September 1975
Third edition, March 1983

Printed in the U.S.A.

Library of Congress Cataloging in Publication Data
Mendenhall, Ruth.
   The Challenge of Rock and Mountain Climbing

   First published in 1969 under title: Introduction to rock & mountain climbing.
   Bibliography: p.
   Includes index.
   1. Mountaineering. 2. Rock climbing. I. Mendenhall, John, joint author. II. Title.
GV200.M46   1975   796.5'22   75-22476
ISBN 0-8117-2146-9

Contents

1

The Sport of Mountain Climbing

TO MOST people mountains are two-dimensional scenery, not much more real than color pictures. To a growing number of men and women, however, each peak is a solid, unique, three-dimensional entity. These few find in the mountains fundamentals that give deep meaning and joy to their lives beyond all ordinary pursuits. These are the ones who climb.

And what is mountain climbing, besides getting to the top of peaks under your own power? The sport has many facets. Nontechnical ascents resemble uphill hikes, often long and strenuous, requiring only energy, outdoor common sense, and the judgment to know where the technical work begins. Technical climbing means using a rope and other equipment on terrain that is hazardous without protection. Beyond the skills and equipment needed, however, it is a sport based largely on the appeal of its splendid environment. Those who do not love and respect the mountains might as well exercise in a gym.

Technical climbing is roughly of two kinds, depending on the terrain. Rock climbing refers to scaling cliffs or boulders with the protection of equipment and special techniques. It may be an exuberant end in itself or an integral part of major ascents. On snow, ice, and glaciers, specialized equipment is also used for assistance and protection. Both rock climbing and snow and ice climbing have their partisans and specialists. Many climbers have an intense interest and competence in both.

Roped climbing, despite a surge of popularity in recent years, is still a poorly understood sport in the United States; it is often deemed sensational or dangerous completely out of proportion to the truth because non-climbers have not the slightest inkling of what is involved. Other sportsmen, such as swimmers, skiers, and ball players, do not become really skilled without aptitude, enjoyment, and long training in techniques and muscle skills. A climber too finds a natural flair helpful, though not indispensable if he is fired with sufficient zeal and desire. To climb safely and well, he must develop skills in specialized, complicated, and sometimes controversial techniques through instruction and practice. He must become familiar with equipment, its evolution, and how to use it. He must gain a detailed knowledge of constantly changing natural conditions. If he seeks really challenging ascents, he must prepare for extreme physical demands. He must possess a high degree of determination, willpower, and tolerance for discomfort. And he must be able to judge his own capacities and those of the people he climbs with. When all this knowledge, drive, and experience are fused together, climbers are safer on potentially dangerous cliffs or glaciers than are careless hikers on a trail.

Who are the people dedicated to so much work for fun and fulfillment? They seem to possess several paradoxical qualities. They gather in organized or unorganized groups for companionship, are usually deeply committed to climbing friendships, and recognize teamwork as a basic ingredient of most safety techniques; but they are individualists, and sometimes loners, who bristle at the very thought of regimentation. Climbing requires an unusual amount of physical fitness and stamina; yet many climbers are students or professionals. The sport demands serious attention to inherent hazards; but climbers are generally humorous and lighthearted. Some are world-famous in the climbing fraternity for their skills and accomplishments; others have the capacity or desire to do only moderate climbs, but enjoy the sport just as much.

Climbers are not of uniform build, age, or sex. The majority are young men in their teens, twenties, and thirties, with a background of outdoor pursuits in which skills adaptable to climbing have been developed; but some start climbing later in life. Women climb with the same motivations and abilities as men; at times they form all-women ropes, expeditions, and clubs. Technical climbing is not ordinarily a sport for children or young teenagers; they have neither the sustained interest nor the endurance necessary, and cannot take a responsible place on the rope until they reach fuller physical development and gain mature judgment.

A climber's role in his sport does not remain static. An enthusiastic and talented beginner learns rapidly. Many people climb for a few years and then, for assorted reasons, give it up. Others find climbing such an absorbing addition to their existence that they pursue it for as long as physical capacities and time permit. Experience, and often endurance, increase for many years. A snow and ice climber may add rock to his repertoire, and a rock specialist may decide that his forte is all-around mountaineering.

People seldom climb half-heartedly, if they climb at all. With the longtime climber, it is not a fleeting interest or a passing thrill, but a dedicated way of life which includes a consuming passion for the mountain environment.

Why do certain individuals climb? Mountain climbing is a varied and challenging sport with great aesthetic and physical appeal. It is usually pursued in wonderful natural surroundings. Each climb is an adventure of such a highly personal nature that anyone who needs to ask "Why?" will never get an answer he fully understands. Climbers seldom try to explain their motivations to non-climbers, though they speculate and philosophize among themselves. The ultimate reason is simply that they like it.

For each potential climber, the sport opens an exciting new world. If it catches your interest, you have a clue as to why. If you want to know how, learn—but learn safely. The real challenge of rock and mountain climbing lies in making ascents with safety, competence, and joy.

2

Rock Climbing for Beginners

A POOR but not uncommon way to start rock climbing is to go off with an old rope and a friend as inexperienced as you are, to try to work out protective techniques on your own. A variation is to pursue this course with the aid of a book. An authoritative climbing book teaches you much *about* climbing; but neither muscle skills nor every nuance of a sport can be learned solely from a book. The only wholly satisfactory way to learn climbing is with experienced, competent companions.

WHO TEACHES ROCK CLIMBING

The first problem is to find knowledgeable climbers who can and will help you attain the beginnings of experience. They may turn up by lucky chance; it is more likely that you will have to go out and hunt for them. This can be done in several ways.

You can hang around climbers (easily identified by ropes, hardware, footgear, and activities) in popular climbing areas; if you exude enough interest, they might offer information and assistance. Climbing schools, large and small, are available in many places. Some high schools and colleges offer climbing and mountaineering courses. Professional guides can be hired near major climbing areas. Probably the best way for most is to look up a climbing club in their school or geographical region. Some clubs specialize in climbing only; some are general outdoor groups that sponsor hikes, ski trips, conservation, etc., as well as mountaineering. Each organization has its own regulations and methods, but almost all offer opportunities for beginners to learn. An important advantage of a club is that members are available, over a period of time, as companions on the numerous and varied ascents that go into making a skilled climber.

GROUNDWORK

If determined, you will find yourself among climbers willing and able to teach you. Your mentor may take you at once on a long climb, where by necessity you quickly find out something about everything. It is more probable that you will spend hours on or near the ground, in an accessible place where large boulders or low cliffs provide a practice area. Here you will be instructed in the basic techniques of safe climbing.

Wear rubber-soled shoes at first, and old clothes suitable for the weather. The group or individual instructing normally contributes the equipment. Beginners must use the ropes, but will find the owners to be fussy about them. Always treat climbing ropes with tender loving care: never step on them, pull them needlessly through the dirt, or drag them over sharp edges.

KNOTS

The protective use of the rope naturally involves tying yourself to it. Knots used by climbers must be bombproof, foolproof, and easy to tie and untie. Many knots fulfill these requirements (and others don't). The particular ones chosen depend on group and individual preference, as well as suitability. The knots described herein cover the needs of beginners, but there are other knots that serve equally well.

Practice your chosen knots with a piece of rope or cord until you can tie them expertly under any conditions. The knots illustrated are drawn the way they look while you are tying them. Left-handed people may prefer to tie them in reverse. Many knots have several names; the most common are used here.

Bowline

For fastening the end of the rope around your waist. It can be tied in several ways; two popular methods are shown in Figure 1. For the method shown in the upper sketch, pass the rope behind you from left to right. Now hold the long or "standing" part of the rope in your left hand, and the short end in the right. With the left hand, make a loop as shown. Doubling this loop will add about 5 percent to the strength of the knot, and is advised. Put the end up through the loop, around the standing end, and back down through the loop. After tying the knot, work it along the rope until the waist loop is really snug. Test and set this knot with a good tug. The bowline tends to loosen with use, and should be safeguarded by tying one or two overhand knots (Figure 2) around the waist loop. Several inches of rope should be left over after the knot is secured. During a climb, check the bowline occasionally, and tighten the waist loop if necessary.

The second method of tying is described below. Either can be used with or without the coil—the results are identical—but for efficiency use one method or the other at first.

Bowline-on-a-Coil

Wind the rope around your waist several times, an arrangement which is more comfortable in case of a fall. Tie the knot around the coil, as illustrated in Figure 1. After step 3, hold onto the short end and jerk the standing end to complete the knot. Test it, and secure with overhands.

BOWLINE

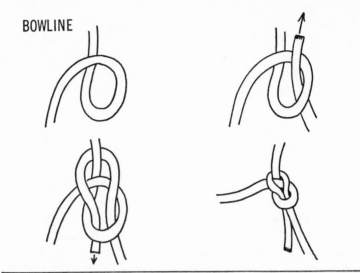

BOWLINE ON COIL

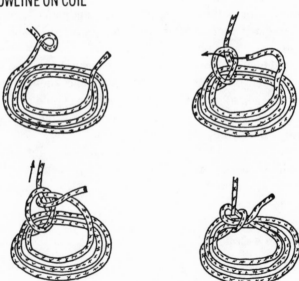

Figure 1.

OVERHAND

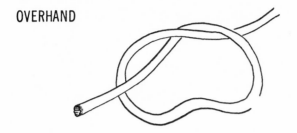

WATER KNOT

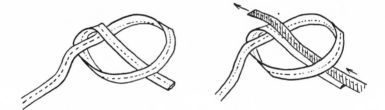

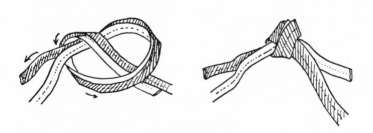

Figure 2.

Overhand

Used to safeguard many other knots from slipping. See Figure 2.

Water Knot or Ring Bend

Used to join the ends of flat nylon webbing or light rope to form slings. Tie an overhand knot loosely in one end, and thread the other end through it in the opposite direction, as shown in Figure 2. With webbing make sure the two parts of the knot lie flat against each other throughout. Set the knot hard, and secure each end with an overhand knot.

Figure Eight Knot

Similar to an overhand knot, but much easier to untie if set hard. See Figure 3. It is tied exactly the same whether in the end of a rope or in a bight (doubled section) of a rope.

Figure Eight Loop

Used to tie into the middle of a rope (Figure 3). Tie a figure eight knot in a bight, leaving a loop large enough to slip over your head and arms. Adjust this loop to a snug fit around your waist by sliding the knot along the rope.

Flemish Bend or Figure Eight Bend

Used to join two ropes of the same or unequal diameters. It resembles the water knot, but is much easier to untie when set (and is also bulkier). Start by tying a loose figure eight knot in one of the rope ends, allowing several extra inches for a safety knot. Thread one end of the second rope through the knot in the opposite direction, as detailed in Figure 3. Make sure that the two ropes lie parallel throughout the knot. Tighten and test by pulling hard in opposite directions on the standing ends of the two ropes; this is especially important if the ropes are of unequal

FIGURE EIGHT

FLEMISH BEND

PRUSSIK

 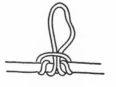 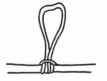

Figure 3.

diameters, as the thinner rope tends to slip out of an improperly formed knot. Secure on each side with one or more overhand knots.

Prussik

An essential aid if, in an emergency, you must climb a rope. The average person is unable to climb a long rope hand over hand; furthermore, ascending your climbing rope in this way would allow slack to accumulate and deprive you of protection.

Prussik knots are formed by twisting slings around a rope which is fixed above you. The knot is illustrated in Figure 3. The climber stands in such loops, which remain in place when weighted but can be slipped up or down when unweighted. The slings should be approximately five or six feet in circumference, varying in size to fit the person and to allow the knots to be in front of the chest for easy handling. All-purpose slings that are best for prussiking are of 6mm perlon. Quarter-inch nylon is satisfactory, but may have to be passed around the rope a third time to improve the grip. Flat webbing slings work, but are harder to manipulate.

A standard technique for ascending a rope with prussiks is to use three slings attached at intervals to the vertical rope, one for a chest loop (for balance) and two footsteps, as shown in Figure 24. The chest loop goes over head and arms. One foot loop should be longer than the other. Balance is improved by tying the slings into smaller loops with a figure eight knot, forming stirrups for the feet. Or, for convenience and versatility, the two lower prussiks may be tied using short slings, with *étriers* (ladderlike slings) clipped into them, as shown in Figure 24.

To ascend, stand with all your weight in the lowest sling, and raise the next one as high as you can step. Transfer your weight to the upper footstep. Raise the chest loop as high as you can for balance. Now pull up the rope hanging below so you can reach the lower foot loop. Slip this loop up as far as possible, using both hands. Stand in it so you can raise the upper foot loop. Repeat this sequence, and up you go! It is strenuous, but gets easier with practice.

CLIMBING WITH THE PROTECTION OF THE ROPE

Once tied in, you can climb, with someone on the rocks above belaying you as a safeguard in case of a fall. The rope is only a protective device, not a handhold. The actual ascent of a cliff somewhat resembles climbing a very steep staircase with scanty irregular treads, some wide, some narrow, some invisible, and most at strange angles. The climber's legs normally do most of the work, with the hands and arms providing balance and some pull. The use of knees is awkward and often prevents smooth climbing, but sometimes seems expeditious despite the sacrifice of skin.

Balance and Momentum

The key to an effortless ascent is balance, the knack of keeping your body weight over the feet, and away from the rock, at exactly the right angle to make full use of whatever support the holds provide. The graceful efficiency of perfect balance is increased manyfold by use of momentum. There are numerous moves where no single hold can support you, but your balance between three or four handholds or footholds gives adequate purchase while you move rhythmically upwards. Whether this skill seems natural or must be learned, it enables you to drift up the rocks instead of lumbering and struggling.

Types of Moves

Friction is an example of pure balance climbing; the resistance between boot soles and rock is all that keeps you from slipping off. Sometimes momentum permits progress where you cannot stand still. Other types of moves for different situations include the mantel, in which you push yourself up on a ledge with the heel of your hand or hands, much like getting out of a swimming pool; chimneying, in which various counter-pressures of back, arms, knees, and feet against opposing walls combine to enable you to wiggle upwards without real holds; various types of hand or foot jams in suitable cracks; and the lieback or layback, in which feet walk up the face of a cliff while hands and arms pull

Figure 4. Climbing cliffs along the Mississippi River. (Courtesy of Resorts International, Denver, Colorado.)

in the opposite direction to create sufficient pressure to keep the feet in place. Some of these special moves are shown in Figures 5 and 6; but you have to feel them in your muscles to believe them.

UPPER BELAYS

You will immediately appreciate the rope's protection when you start to climb. And an absolutely necessary step for participation in roped climbing is acquiring the skill to protect other climbers. Giving an upper belay to someone climbing below you is an introduction to protecting a climber above in more advanced work.

To give an upper belay, sit down in a safe spot, feet apart and firmly braced. You should face the climber, and be anchored (tied) to a *sound* rock, tree, piton, or chocks so you cannot possibly be pulled off; deaths have occurred due to failure of an anchor. The rope coming up from the climber below is passed around your hips. Both hands hold the rope, one on each side of your body. The proper position is illustrated in Figure 7.

The hand on the climber's end guides, feels, and takes in the rope as the climber ascends. The other hand holds the weight in case of a fall. The friction of the rope around your hips makes this surprisingly easy. Take in the rope by moving the "feeling" hand toward the body. At the same time extend the belay hand away from the body, pulling the rope with it. Quickly slide both hands along the rope to their former positions. The belay hand in particular must never let go of the rope; if you have trouble sliding it along the slack rope, the "feeling" hand can momentarily do double duty by grasping the belaying part of the rope between thumb and fingertips to provide a little tension. Continue to take in rope.

While you are learning to belay, the climber below should call "Testing!" before he starts to climb. Reply "Test!" and he will give a gradual but strong pull so you can gain an idea of how it would feel if he fell off.

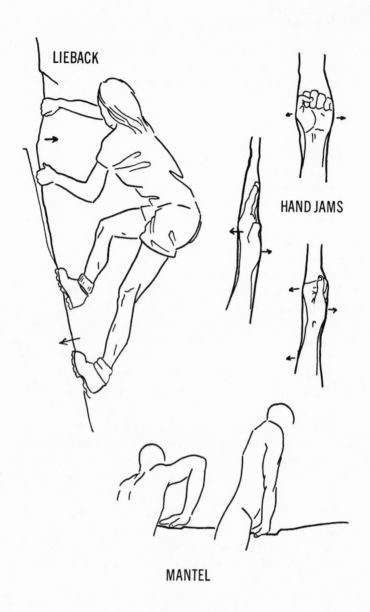

LIEBACK

HAND JAMS

MANTEL

Figure 5.

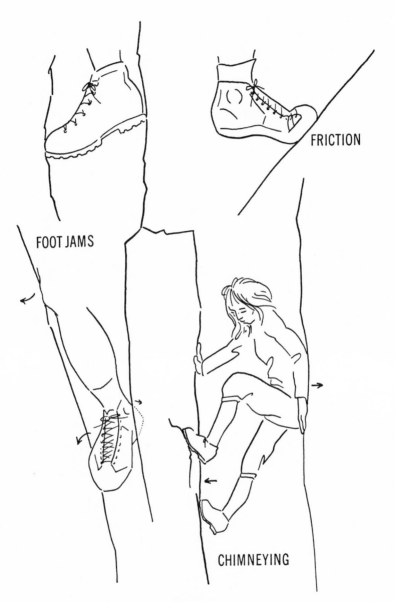

FRICTION

FOOT JAMS

CHIMNEYING

Figure 6.

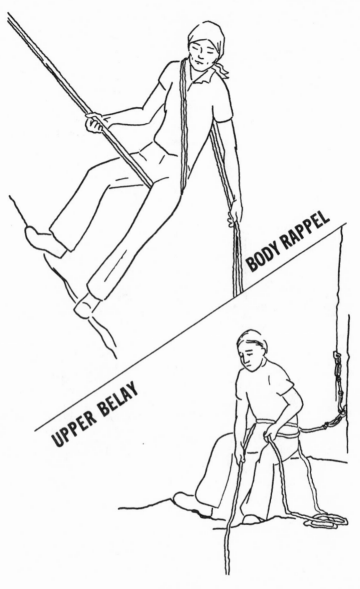

BODY RAPPEL

UPPER BELAY

Figure 7.

HANDLING THE ROPE SMOOTHLY

While belaying, you must watch the rope carefully. Lay the part you pull up in a pile, preferably within reach, and in a place where it is unlikely to snag on anything or knock off rocks. Keep the rope just tight enough so you can feel the climber, but don't pull. Your guiding hand tells you how fast to take in rope.

The person climbing also has a responsibility toward the rope. He must keep it free of kinks, notice if it snags or catches, and make sure he does not overclimb the rope. If slack accumulates, he should slow down or stop until the rope is again taut.

CLIMBING SIGNALS

Climbers on the same rope are frequently out of each other's sight and may be almost out of earshot as well. Yet it is essential that each knows what the other is doing. A set of verbal signals has been pretty well standardized among climbers; but in a new group, check out what signals are used. Routine signals in roped climbing are:

Belayer: "Belay on!"

Climber: "Climbing!"

Belayer: "Climb!"

Climber, when he wants the belayer to take in more rope, or take it in faster: "Rope!" or "Up rope!"

Climber, when he wants the belayer to support him on the rope: "Tension!"

Climber, when he needs less tension, or extra slack for maneuvering, descending, throwing the rope, etc.: "Slack!"

Climber, to warn belayer, "Prepare for fall!" or "Falling!"

Either, if a rock (or other object) falls: "Rock!"

Climber, when he is in a safe position near the belayer (or elsewhere): "Belay off!"

Belayer: "Belay off!"

Except perhaps for "rope" and "slack," signals are usually repeated by the person they are meant for as a confirmation that he has heard, understood, and is taking appropriate action. You may have to shout repeatedly, as loudly as you can; but do not assume that a vital signal has been heard until you get an answer.

Even moderate winds can make it impossible to hear shouts, and on steep rocks the climbers often cannot see each other; varying numbers of tugs on the rope can transmit signals, but expect some frustrations.

LEARNING TO RAPPEL*

Climbers have developed several methods of descending steep rocks by sliding down a rope which has been doubled around a fixed point. This is called "rappelling," "roping down," or sometimes "abseiling" from the German. The instructor commonly sets the rappel for beginners; how to do it is explained in Chapter 3.

You will probably begin with a simple body rappel, sometimes called the *Dülfersitz,* with a belay for safety. This basic rappel is generally modified for long descents, but should be known by everyone because it requires no equipment except the rope.

To get into the rappel, stand below the point around which the rope is doubled. Face the cliff and straddle the doubled rope. Take hold of the doubled rope behind you, and bring it forward across the left hip. Pull it up *across* your chest, and backwards over your right shoulder. The doubled rope now hangs down behind you. Grasp it with your left (lower) hand, palm forward and thumb downward. This rappel position is illustrated in Figure 7. The lower hand supports your weight, holds you into the rope, and must *never* let go. The right (upper) hand holds onto the rope above for balance, and is the one to be used for any necessary adjustments. A left-handed person may prefer to reverse the arrangement; but everyone should eventually become ambidextrous at rappelling.

Once in the rope, lean backwards. Your body should be at about a forty-five-degree angle to the rock, knees bent slightly and feet twenty-four to thirty-six inches apart for balance on the varying inclines. Looking down frequently over your left shoulder to see where you are going, walk backwards or sideways down the cliff. The rope slides slowly through your hands and over your body. The points of greatest friction, where the rope passes over

*Rappel is pronounced with the accent on the last syllable.

hip and shoulder, become very hot if you go too fast; extra padding may be advisable at these points. The lower hand controls the speed of descent; nothing is gained by gripping frantically with the upper hand. At the bottom, make sure your footing is good, and step out of the rope. Call "Off rappel!" to those above.

COILING THE ROPE

One of the beginner's duties may be to learn how to coil the climbing rope for carrying and storage. Methods vary. A popular one is the Mountaineer's Coil, quick and easy to coil and uncoil, illustrated in Figure 8. With one hand gather up successive coils about five feet in circumference and place them neatly in the other hand. Don't fight the rope if it twists into a figure eight. Bend the starting end back on itself for a foot or so and preserve this loop with the holding hand. Wrap the last few feet of the other end closely and firmly around the coils where they are held together. Pass the end through the loop. Pull both ends tight, and tie a square knot for extra firmness.

CLIMBING EQUIPMENT

Soon after you start climbing, some personal equipment is needed. It varies somewhat according to areas and the people with whom you climb. Observe what your companions are using and ask their advice. Go slow about buying equipment until you know what you really want and need. Many sporting goods stores handle or specialize in mountaineering supplies. There are also excellent mail-order sources which publish informative catalogs. If you become seriously interested in rock climbing, you should gradually acquire some or all of the equipment discussed below; additional equipment that you will need if you climb on snow and ice is discussed in Chapter 4.

When you start to climb second and to lead, to fend for yourself and take some responsibility for others in the party, you will need and want more equipment of your own. You will have studied and used various kinds of ropes, slings, and hardware, and listened to endless discussions. Thus you can make a choice without

depending entirely on the advice of sales people (many are climbers but not all), or being unduly tempted by unneeded gadgets.

Rock Climbing Shoes

Specialized shoes are a basic requirement. While heavy boots
are essential for mixed rock and snow climbing, rock shoes are
much superior for serious rock work. The best styles have high-
friction rubber soles, with the rubber extending up the toes, heels,
and sides for efficiency in jam cracks and for reinforcement. These
shoes should fit snugly over one pair of light socks. A tight fit
aids edging, but shoes that are too snug become painful for walking.

Harness

Tying the rope around your waist is satisfactory for practice
climbing while belayed from above, but a seat harness provides
far greater safety and convenience in real ascents. The addition
(not substitution) of a chest harness increases safety, especially
if one hangs awhile, but chest harnesses are rarely seen in North
America.

Tie the rope to the harness with a bowline, preferably doubled.
Many experienced climbers tie the rope to a locking carabiner (or
two carabiners with reversed gates) and clip it onto the harness;
this is somewhat less safe than tying directly to the harness,
because of the sharp bend of the rope at the carabiner(s).

Swami Belt

Some climbers wear a fifteen-foot length of one-inch nylon webbing wound around the waist and secured snugly with a water
knot.

A better and safer arrangement is to make leg loops in the
webbing to keep the waist loop from riding up around the ribs in
a fall. Use one-inch webbing about twenty-five feet long. Tie two
leg loops that fit (not tightly) at crotch level, using an overhand
knot. One loop should be about five feet from an end of the
webbing, the other six or seven inches farther from the short end.

Put your right leg through the loop that is closest to the short end of the webbing, and your left leg through the other loop. Pull the loops up to your crotch. Run the long end of the webbing counterclockwise around your back, through the left loop, around your back again, and through the right-hand leg loop. Then wind both ends of the webbing around your waist as many times as the length permits. Tie the ends together with a water knot, and secure them with overhand knots. Attach the climbing rope to the Swami in the same way as to a harness.

Climbing Rope

The rope must be of synthetic material (nylon or perlon) for strength and elasticity, and should be one manufactured especially for mountaineering. There are two chief types, either laid (twisted) or sheath (kernmantle) construction. A hard-lay nylon rope serves well for a beginning or occasional climber. Its advantages are lower cost and ease of inspection for damage; its disadvantages are its stiffness (which causes more drag through carabiners) and its tendency to kink.

A kernmantle rope, of perlon, has a core of continuous filaments which provide strength, and a woven sheath (in a variety of colors) to protect the core. It is lighter in weight, and is preferred for long serious rock climbs because it creates less rope drag than a laid rope.

Most climbers use kernmantle rope, 10.5 or 11mm in diameter and 150 feet in length, for rock climbs. Climbers using laid rope generally select $7/16$ inch diameter rope 150 feet long. Shorter ropes are convenient and save weight on high peaks and glaciers. "Big wall" climbs have few belay points, and 165-foot lengths are preferred.

Slings or Runners

Loops used with many types of protection and for other purposes. They may be ready-made or constructed from flat nylon webbing, usually one inch wide, or from 9mm perlon rope. They vary from about three to eight feet in circumference after the knot

MOUNTAINEERS' COIL

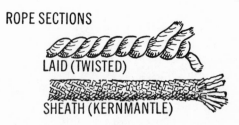

ROPE SECTIONS

LAID (TWISTED)

SHEATH (KERNMANTLE)

Figure 8.

is tied; longer ones can be formed quickly by joining two or more slings, as shown in Figure 12. All perlon and nylon sling material, when cut, should immediately have the ends fused with flame to prevent raveling. Tie the ends together with a water knot, set hard, and secure with overhand knots. Always carry several assorted slings with you.

Most climbers use a sling for carrying hardware. Instead of being knotted, this sling (''hardware rack'') can have the ends overlapped and sewn together thoroughly, with strong thread. The lack of a knot is comfortable, and lets the hardware slide freely. But *never* use this sewn sling for any other purpose as it may not be strong enough.

Carabiners

Snaplinks of aluminum alloy, usually oval or roughly pear-shaped, about four inches long. There is a spring gate opening on one

Figure 9. Kernmantle climbing ropes are lighter in weight and preferred for
more serious climbs. (Courtesy of Forrest Mountaineering, Denver,
Colorado.)

side, sometimes with a screw lock. Carabiners are used to connect
the climbing rope with a sling which is attached to a rock, tree
or chock; or with the eye of a piton. They also are used to carry
hardware or rig slings, and for other purposes. Carabiners in use
are shown in Figures 11, 12, 13, and 14. Keep carabiners out of
dust and grit, and never oil them since oil collects grime.

Chocks or Nuts

Artificial chock stones (usually aluminum alloy) that come in
various shapes and sizes to wedge or jam into cracks for protection in difficult climbing, or even in severe moves. They are threaded
with slings of nylon webbing, perlon rope, or wire cable. Several

types are shown in Figure 10 and their use is discussed in detail in Chapter 3.

Chock Picks

Essential for removing many chocks. Manufactured picks are best, but properly modified shelf brackets will work.

Pitons*

Metal blades or angles, with an eye in the head, also for protection and aid in severe climbs. They are usually of chrome-molybdenum steel alloy ("chromolly") and are made in many shapes and sizes. They are driven into cracks in the rock with a piton hammer. Their use is discussed in Chapter 3. Beginners

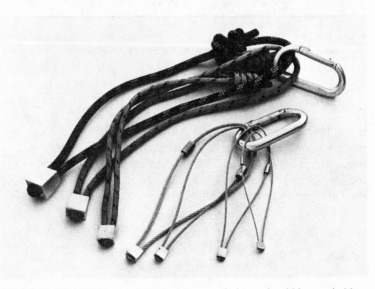

Figure 10. Chocks, in a variety of shapes and sizes, should be carried by all climbers.

*Piton is pronounced "pee-tonn."

should not acquire pitons, hammers, and keepers. Please see discussion of chocks vs. pitons in Chapter 3.

Hammer

Its main function is to drive and remove pitons. Secondary uses are cleaning cracks, testing holds, setting or removing occasional stubborn chocks, and as a general tool. Hammers of both American and European make are available in a wide price range. Handles are of hickory, steel, or fiberglass. The head is square and has a wedge or point opposite. Choose one that feels balanced in your hand and is heavy enough for a real wallop.

The hammer must be fitted with a sling to guard against dropping. It may come so equipped; if not, thread the hole in the handle's end with a piece of nylon cord long enough for a loop that goes around your neck and under one arm, with enough additional cord to permit full reach with either hand. The hammer is usually carried in a plastic or leather belt holster.

Piton Keeper or Retriever

A lightweight clip fastened to you with a light cord or an old carabiner on a sling, to prevent dropping pitons while driving or removing.

Helmets and Hats

Due to the number of head injuries in climbing (both from falling rock and from injuries sustained in leader falls), hard hats or helmets are now commonly seen on climbers. They are sold in mountaineering shops. Necessary features include a good fit; a dependable and adjustable chin strap; the manufacturer's name; and information as to strength under impact. Helmets weigh between one and one and a half pounds, and come in many colors.

An ordinary felt hat is preferable to climbing bareheaded. It cushions the head from minor blows, shades from sunburn, protects glasses in rain, and keeps dirt and sun out of the eyes. A felt hat also can be stuffed inside your shirt as insulation against rope burn in rappelling. However, bareheadedness is sometimes chosen for the sheer freedom of it.

Rucksack

A small summit pack, often of light tough nylon, is needed to keep your stuff together and to transport it to the start of the climb. It is also usually needed on the climb, and the least experienced member of the party, usually climbing third, may have the honor of carrying his party's supplies.

Clothing

Temperatures are often far hotter or colder on the rocks than on the ground. Climate, season, storm, and whether the climb will be in sun or shade should be considered. Don't forget the skin- and fabric-grinding effects of rock. Take extra boots and socks for long approaches. Rock shoes tight enough for climbing are often miserable for hiking, particularly downhill. Pants or knickers should be loose enough so you can raise your foot to waist level.

Miscellaneous

Carry a pocketknife. Supply sunglasses and sunburn lotion if required—the glare on light rock resembles that on water. If you wear prescription glasses, make sure they can't fall off. A wristwatch is vulnerable to damage.

Don't forget that as time goes by, ropes, slings, pitons, and so on, may become unsafe; scrutinize occasionally for wear or damage, and replace if you find signs of weakness.

CONSECUTIVE CLIMBING ON MULTI-PITCH ROUTES

Having practiced the basic techniques and acquired some equipment, you are ready for multi-pitch climbing. A pitch is the distance climbed between belay spots, generally about 50 to 130 feet.

Routes

Climbs are not made just anywhere on the cliff. A route usually goes up a portion of the cliff or mountain that has been broken by natural forces into connecting cracks, ledges, chimneys, flakes, etc., which provide handholds and footholds, niches for suitable chock or piton placement, and belay stances. Routes viewed from a distance may appear dauntingly steep, but a side view usually reveals an easier angle. Frequently you find more holds when climbing than there appeared to be from a distance; but the opposite may also be true.

Climbing Parties

A "rope" means not only the object itself, but also the team that climbs tied together for protection. The usual number on a rope is two or three. As a beginner, you will probably start consecutive climbing as third at the end of the rope, and can learn what is involved without much responsibility except for your own climbing. The second man will protect both the leader and the third. After the rope is made up, the climbers go to the foot of the chosen route. The climbing ropes are uncoiled and laid in a loose pile (to prevent snarls), hardware is adjusted, and the climbers tie in.

Order of Climbing

The second man takes his belay position, and the leader climbs. The leader may place protection occasionally; when he reaches the next belay spot, he stops, prepares to belay, and calls to the second to climb. You as third have so far done nothing. When the second starts to climb, watch the rope going up to him, make sure it does not snag, and perhaps pay it out. When the second reaches the leader, he belays the leader up another pitch. You, the third man, are again doing nothing. But be ready to climb as soon as the word comes down—and don't forget the rucksack.

When the leader is at the top of the second pitch, the second man turns his attention to the third man. If there is extra rope between you, he pulls it up; you should notify him when it is all up. Signals are exchanged (skipping the "Test" part), and you start to climb. If you reach a chock or piton, you will see that the rope is running through a carabiner snapped into a sling or eye. Stop in as convenient a place as you can, remove the rope from the carabiner, remove the carabiner, and snap it into your waist loop or hardware rack. For your future information, notice just how and where the leader placed his protection.

Remove the protection (methods are discussed under chock and piton techniques in Chapter 3), and call "Climbing!" to let your belayer know you are moving again. When you reach the second man, you will probably find he is anchored in with a sling or section of rope to a rock, tree, chocks, or piton. (Anchors are discussed more fully in Chapter 3.) Tie yourself on in the same way. Hand the hardware you have collected to the second man, who takes it along for the leader's use.

Be attentive to your ropemates' actions, needs, and instructions. Do not move until you receive the signal to climb. Watch and tend the rope. Once on the climb, it is a good idea for the third to belay the second; it gives practice in rope handling and is an extra safeguard for all. Remember to remove the anchor before starting the next pitch.

Tips for Beginners

A few pointers may help on your first long climbs. Concentrate on the climbing. Watch the climbers ahead of you; it is very helpful to know which holds they use, and how, even though you may climb the pitch differently. While climbing, look for holds; feel for them; try them with your hands and feet in different positions. Make all possible use of small holds close together to minimize the effort of hauling yourself up. Climb quickly. Many holds are fine for a swift smooth passage but not as a stopping place. Rest (if necessary) on large holds where you can relax.

A few cautions may also be of help. You will probably be too busy to notice the empty spaces below, known as "exposure," or you may find it exhilarating. But if it bothers you, look back at the rock and the rope, and remember that you are well-protected. Check your waist loop occasionally. Test handholds that might come off; if they are loose, find others. Be very careful not to dislodge rocks with feet, hands, or rope. If a rock does fall, yell "Rock! Rock!" for the benefit of anyone below. If you see or hear one coming from above, get your head up against the cliff, into a crack, or under an overhang—and be quick about it. If you cannot take cover, watch the rock and duck at the last second. Whenever possible, keep out from under climbers above.

Even if the climbing seems hairy and the chocks or pitons won't budge, refrain from complaint. Grunt, ask advice, or make jokes—but don't claim you can't! Don't talk too much; it distracts your companions and sometimes annoys them. Listen to the more experienced; there is still much to learn.

3

Gaining Experience on Rock

HAVING practiced the basic techniques of rock climbing and tried a multi-pitch ascent, you have reached a sort of crossroads. Some beginners, of course, decide the sport is not for them, though its elementary safety measures may prove useful on non-technical ascents. Others, swept away by the sheer delight of rock climbing, are affected as if a sort of revelation had changed their outlook on life. It has.

THE ADVANCED BEGINNER AND INTERMEDIATE CLIMBER

If you are among the converts, your beginner's role as passive third on the rope will not last long. With the basic know-how, you will probably begin to belay the leader on easy climbs. In due time, depending on your ability, temperament, and enthusiasm, you will start leading. It is well to make initial leads on familiar climbs that are easy for you, with an experienced second.

By this time, too, additional equipment and a full familiarity with its uses are required.

Expert techniques and good judgment are best developed during a period in which you are a sort of apprentice or understudy. You should make diverse climbs with many climbers, giving thoughtful attention to all that occurs. You should progress from easy to difficult climbs at your own tempo. It will take at least one or two climbing seasons, perhaps several or many, before you reach your top potential as a climber. Whether you turn out to be an average or outstanding rock climber has little correlation with your enjoyment of the sport. In any event, both ascent and descent are more complex than they seem from the comparatively carefree tail end of the rope.

NUMBER OF CLIMBERS ON A ROPE

A roped climbing party is routinely made up of either two or three people, preferably two on rock. More than three is too time-consuming and cumbersome to be justified except in an emergency.

The Three-Man Rope

A rope of three may be chosen for reasons such as companionship, safety, photography, instruction, or shortage of rope leaders. The third man may be inexperienced, but is not necessarily so. He may be an alternate leader who swings leads with the fellow at the other end, the least experienced person being tied in the middle. In such cases, the usual climbing order is changed: the third joins the others at each belay stance, to take his turn at leading, or to belay the leader if the second is a novice.

Though three climbers occasionally tie into one long rope, it is preferable for them to use two ropes. The middle man ties into the rope that goes to the leader, leaving an end of about thirty inches which is joined to the second rope with a Flemish bend. The knot should be guarded by overhand knots, and should be within a few inches of his body or it will interfere when carabiners are reached.

The Two-Man Rope

Two on a rope climb considerably faster than three. Speed is not the primary aim of climbing, of course; but it is essential on long or difficult routes, and smooth fast climbing is pure pleasure.

The order of climbing may take either of two forms: (1) The two may be of equal or nearly equal ability, who lead alternate pitches. Or one may be an intermediate climber gaining experience who leads the less difficult sections. In either case, the leader brings the second up to his ledge. There the second climbs past the belayer to lead the next pitch. This speeds up climbing because transfer of hardware, rope handling, and changing anchors and belay positions are minimized. (2) One may do all or most of the leading, either from ability or desire. The climbers may be unequal in experience, one may be teaching the other, or they may form a team that almost always climbs together with one leading and the other seconding.

On two-man ropes the second performs all the functions of the third as well as those specifically the obligations of the second.

RELATIONSHIP BETWEEN ROPE LEADER AND SECOND MAN

Both the rope leader and the second man are essential parts of a climbing rope, and should understand each other's duties and responsibilities in order to climb as a team with the greatest safety, efficiency, and pleasure.

Generally the rope leader has served a stint as second while gaining the personal insight and experience needed for competent leading. Sometimes he is a climber of such agility, drive, and daring that he never spent much time as second-man "apprentice" climber. However, every leader at least occasionally climbs second, and hence understands that man's position.

The second may be an experienced climber who, whether he leads or not, knows exactly what the leader is doing, and his needs. The second may be instead a climber of limited experience, who must be responsive enough to the leader's requirements to learn to protect him, and do it well.

LEADER'S RESPONSIBILITIES

The word "leader" commonly has two connotations in climbing. The term may refer to a climber with sufficient experience and judgment to take charge of a group, regardless of whether he goes first on the rope. However, in this book it is used primarily to refer to the rope leader, who is not invariably the person best qualified to make decisions for the group. The climbing leader is generally casual and democratic and rarely pulls rank on his fellowman.

What to Take on a Climb

The leader should know or find out enough about the prospective route to choose the equipment. A view of the climb, friends' advice, or a guidebook will indicate the length and difficulty of the route, and what protective equipment is apt to be required. Surplus hardware may be carried for emergencies, but a great deal extra simply adds undesirable weight and the temptation to overprotect. Necessary food, water, and clothing should be included. The leader should make sure other rope members have hammers (if required), and at least a minimum of other equipment.

Leader's Special Problems

A leader's position differs from that of his ropemates' primarily in his lack of the almost perfect protection afforded by an upper belay. If the leader falls unprotected, he falls at least twice the distance between himself and his belayer. After he has placed protection, he theoretically can fall only twice the distance between himself and the protection—if it doesn't come out. This principle is illustrated in Figure 15. As he climbs, the leader has the rope's weight and friction to pull against. He must choose the route. The leader does not regard these conditions as drawbacks; he exults in them as adding zest and challenge to the climb.

Rope Management

When you are leading, keep your belayer sufficiently informed to help him with rope handling. After placing your first protection, signal him to make sure he knows the pull will now come up instead of down if you fall. Once out of the belayer's sight, keep him informed of your activities to help him handle the rope smoothly. Keep an eye on the rope behind you. If it catches, ask for slack and try to free it. Sometimes the belayer can help. Arrange your protection so the rope runs through it without unnecessary friction; if friction becomes too great, haul the rope up a few feet before each move. If you need temporary support on the rope when protection is at your level or above, call "Tension!" If a fall seems imminent, warn the belayer.

USE OF EQUIPMENT FOR LEADER PROTECTION

An experienced leader develops a fairly reliable feel for what he can climb without needing protection and in what places he would prefer to have it. Reduced to the simplest terms, protection is placed below sections where the leader thinks he might peel off, or where a fall would be excessively long and serious. It is placed before he finds his position too precarious, and if possible from a reasonably comfortable stance to avoid exhaustion. There are other considerations in placing protection. One is the size and experience of the belayer. Another is the type of pitch; for instance, on a traverse, protection may spare both the leader and the last man a long swinging pendulum. Another consideration is the possible landing place; a sliding fall in a trough will often be easier on the protective system, but harder on the climber, than a free fall. While learning, you will probably want somewhat more than the standard amount of protection; but if you cannot lead a climb without far more than is customary for the route, descend and gain more experience on easier routes.

Types of Protection

In the early days of roped ascents, climbers relied for protection on natural features such as chock stones and horns, around which they belayed their ropes. Such natural features, combined with slings, are still used. Next came pitons, first makeshift and then especially for climbing. They were originally fashioned of soft iron, but in recent years have been made almost exclusively of hard steel alloys. Pitons were quickly adopted in some countries, but scorned in others (particularly Great Britain). Finally they were almost universally accepted. Where there are no cracks, climbers sometimes use various kinds of expansion bolts driven into blank rock for protection and aid. Slings are an integral part of most protective systems.

The newest protective devices, chocks, or nuts, have in recent years gained great popularity as replacements for pitons. The concept was developed in Britain as an imitation of natural chock stones. It evolved from artificially placed stones to the similar use of hexagonal machine nuts. Chocks (also called nuts) made especially for climbers were the next logical step. Their forms, sizes, and functions have become varied and sophisticated and their use widespread.

Chocks vs. Pitons

Chocks have become the standard protection on rock. Pitons are normally carried only when adverse conditions such as ice-filled cracks, nocturnal rappels, or a rescue are anticipated.

Pitons damage and deface the rock, and may pry out flakes and unstable blocks. Wear and tear on rock is not a problem with chocks. This characteristic has led to the term "clean climbing" being applied to climbs done with slings and chocks only. Chocks are lighter to carry, and quicker and less fatiguing to place and remove than pitons. Many climbers feel that chocks have been proven as safe as pitons when their proper use has been mastered by a person who knows his limits. Perhaps an overriding factor among enthusiasts is that chocks add a challenging and fascinating new skill to the climbing "game" for those who believe a climb done clean is aesthetically superior, and provides more sheer pleasure in the sport.

It should be emphasized that some climbs require no protection at all, and this type of route is excellent for a climber's first leads. But when needed, both pitons and chocks must be placed with skill. The shock of a fall is absorbed almost simultaneously by the climber, the rope, the carabiners, the slings, chocks and/or pitons, and the belayer. If a chock or piton fails, the entire se-

Figure 11. Use of natural features for protection.

quence of protection is endangered. Much practice is necessary to achieve expertise in placing protection. A few pointers will help the beginner.

Chock Techniques

An ample supply of chocks, in a variety of shapes, should be carried. "Friends®" are chocks having four cams that will hold even in out-flaring cracks. However, they are quite bulky and expensive, and use is justified only on some severe climbs.

Except for Friends®, chocks must be equipped with wire or slings threaded through their holes. The wired ones come ready for use; those that take slings may or may not. If you install your own slings, use the largest runner that will go through the holes with reasonable ease. Either perlon rope or nylon webbing is used. Rope wears longer, but webbing fits better into thin cracks. The size of the sling is often the limiting factor on the strength of chocks; anything smaller than 8 or 9mm perlon or one-inch webbing (both for large chocks) is insufficient for beginners. Melt both ends of the sling material. Shape one end into a point and put it through the holes. Join the ends with a water knot; jam the knot hard. Carry chocks with long slings around the neck and one arm, or those with short slings clipped to the hardware rack.

Placement and removal of chocks may be quick and easy; but placement, especially, requires finesse and close attention to rock structure to ensure good protection. Study the rock. For practice, use chocks freely anywhere you think they will hold, whether or not you need them for safety. Some good and bad placements are shown in Figure 12. Look for a vertical crack that flares out behind the opening; try the largest chock that will go in its narrowest way. Turn the chock inside the crack (with fingers and sling). When its position seems good, set and test it with a hard jerk. In both placing and testing, the dependability of the chock is paramount, but its removability must also be considered. Make sure it is placed within reach so it won't slip into an irretrievable position, and don't set it harder than really necessary.

When the chock is placed, clip the rope in with a carabiner, and climb past with care. Don't be too disconcerted if you look down and see that one or several nuts have been pulled upward

CHOCK PLACEMENT

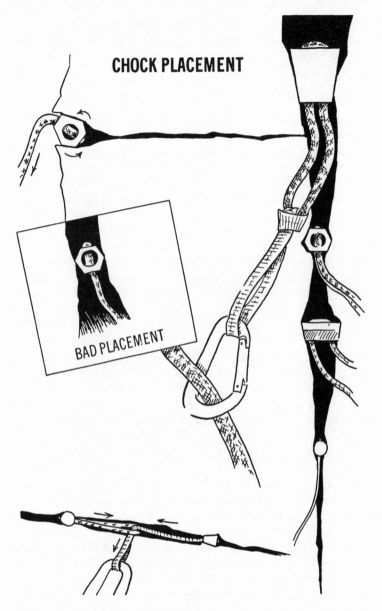

BAD PLACEMENT

Figure 12.

Figure 13. Placement and removal of chocks requires some finesse, and techniques to use them adeptly should be studied well.

by the rope, fallen out of cracks, and slid down the rope. If they were well placed, they probably would have held a fall until you placed more protection (which you should have done before they came out). However, minimize their tendency to be pulled out by adding runners to all chocks having wire or short slings; also to the slings of other chocks if this helps keep the rope moving in as straight a line as possible. Wired nuts are particularly sensitive to rope pull, and should be fitted with generous runners in use.

As you become more skilled, you will appreciate the endless sizes and shapes of cracks, and become adept at matching chocks to them. Sloping, horizontal, even outward-flaring cracks can be used, as well as other formations. The chock at the upper left in Figure 12 stays in place in an outward-flaring crack because of rotation under stress (camming). Sometimes when a single chock won't stay in, a second one can be placed in the same or a nearby crack; the two slings pull against each other and thus force the chocks to stay in; the principle is illustrated at the bottom of Figure 12. Unless a chock is very sound, don't depend on only one—place several on a difficult pitch.

Two sound chocks can be used for a belay anchor if they protect in every direction from which a pull could come.

To remove a chock, first inspect its position and the rock with care. Next try delicate wiggling, usually sufficient to coax it out. A pull may seem necessary, but may also result in jamming it in a worse position. Most climbers carry chock picks. A light hammer is sometimes useful, often in conjunction with the extractor, even if pitons have not been in use. In extraction, take care not to damage the sling. Make every effort to get chocks out; one virtue of chocks is their lack of impact on the rock—but indestructible aluminum chocks plus bright nylon slings do not improve the landscape.

Piton Techniques

To drive, select a crack that is a sound cleavage in solid rock. Ideally, the crack should narrow gradually for several inches behind the opening. Pick a piton to fit the crack, preferably a portion of the crack that is a little wider than its adjacent parts. A half to three-quarters of the piton blade should go into the crack before driving. Any thin crack, horizontal, vertical, or sloping, will take horizontal pitons. Wide cracks call for angles, and still wider ones for bongs. The eye of a horizontal should be downward unless the rock formation prevents; an angle or bong should have the open side downward in horizontal cracks and sideways in vertical cracks. Various pitons in place are shown in Figure 14.

While driving, listen to the sound of hammer blows on the piton. If the rock is good and crack and piton compatible, each blow rings with an increasingly high pitch. A dull hollow sound often indicates a loose piton. It should go in hard up to the eye, leaving room to insert the carabiner. If a piton wiggles, goes in too easily, or sticks out too far, remove it and try another piton, or look for a better crack. If a piton goes in only a short distance, seems sound, and no other placement is possible, you can reduce leverage by placing a short sling ("hero loop") around the blade close to the rock for use instead of the eye (Figure 14). Test pitons with a medium blow in each direction parallel to the crack, and sometimes further by jerking on them with the rope. Pitons *must* be sound; secondarily, they should not be overdriven, as removal becomes time-consuming or impossible. A succession of pitons should be placed in as straight a line as possible to reduce rope friction; slings used as links between piton and rope can often help keep the rope from binding (Figure 14).

For several reasons, pitons are usually removed and re-used. The weight is a factor; the same piton may be needed again; thrift enters in. Climbing etiquette demands leaving the rocks in their natural state. To extract a piton, hammer it forcefully back and forth as far as it will go, until you can pull it out. If possible, strike the body rather than the eye region. If your position is too shaky or exhausting, call "Tension!" and your belayer can partially support you on the rope; signal "Climbing!" when you are ready to go on. Pitons can be stubborn, but with time, persistence, and might, most do come out.

Occasionally pitons are left in for the use of the second rope, to save time, or because it seemed they would not come out. Those found in place should be tested before use, as they often become unsafe from corrosion or from changes in the crack. Remove such strays if you can. But in areas where pitons (often

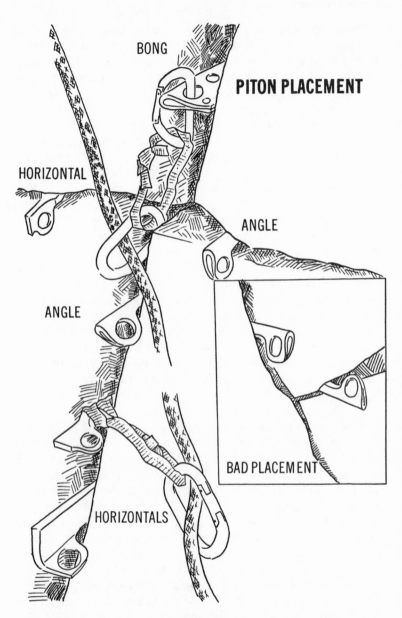

PITON PLACEMENT

BONG

HORIZONTAL

ANGLE

ANGLE

BAD PLACEMENT

HORIZONTALS

Figure 14.

soft iron ones) have purposely been placed on standard routes as fixtures, to save wear and tear on cracks, leave them in as local custom requires.

Carabiner Handling

After clipping the carabiner onto a sling or into the eye of a piton, invert the carabiner so the gate is outward from the rock and the gate opening is down. When putting the rope through the carabiner, be sure it goes in a direction that permits it to run free as you climb. This is always important to reduce rope drag, but especially so when a series of carabiners is used. If protection is placed in a deep recess out of line with other protection, or in any position that causes the rope to bind or to pull over a sharp edge, use slings or additional carabiners to allow the rope to run more freely, as suggested in Figures 11 and 12.

Direct Aid

Pitches, moves, or almost entire climbs where the holds are inadequate are sometimes climbed by using pitons, chocks, or expansion bolts, fitted with ladderlike slings (*étriers*) for footsteps. Mechanical ascenders such as Jumars, which grip the rope, are sometimes used by all but the leader for climbing the rope. These methods may save time, or permit ascents otherwise impossible. But they are not acceptable as a substitute for good climbing, and are seldom needed or used except in advanced and specialized rock work. The term "free" means climbing done without aid.

THE SECOND MAN

The leader's protective devices in team climbing are useless without the skills of the second man. The second has an assortment of duties, of which by far the most important is safeguarding the leader. For this function he should be prepared by instruction and practice. Figure 15 shows the second giving one type of "leader belay," and will clarify the following discussion.

Types of Leader Falls

There are two types of leader falls: (1) A fall from above the belayer, without protective devices in place. The pull on the belayer is downward, and the techniques used in holding the fall are somewhat like those for an upper belay—modified to accommodate a much greater force. (2) A fall from above after the rope has been clipped into piton, chock, or sling. The essential difference to the belayer is that he receives an upward, rather than a downward, pull.

Practice in Belaying the Leader

In spite of all the effort going into protection, leaders do not often fall off in actual climbing. You may go through your entire climbing career without once having to field a leader. However, if a fall comes, the demands on the belayer are so severe, and his reaction so vital, that holding leader falls should be practiced diligently before they are actually needed. Otherwise, you can hardly conceive of the jolt you may get—or, surprisingly, how well you can hold moderate falls when you know how. Though you might well succeed unrehearsed, it is one thing you should not count on learning as you go along.

Two or three people, or a group, can practice the technique with simple setups such as a very sound piton above an overhang, or from the lowest limb of a suitable tree. One climber, pretending to be a falling leader, can jump off while another catches him on the rope. A safer method (though more trouble) is to replace the climber with a dead weight, such as a log, large tire, or bucket of concrete that has a bent reinforcing bar embedded in it for attaching it to the rope. The object need not be as heavy as a person. For one thing, unlike a living body, it does not absorb part of the shock; and for another, more slack can be safely accumulated in the rope. For practicing with a dead weight, use an old rope retired from active climbing—never risk taking the stretch out of a good one. The learning belayer should be positioned and anchored safely beyond the line of fall. Except for this precaution, the techniques are much the same as on a climb.

Belay Stance of Second Man on Climb

In selecting belay spots, there are several considerations which should be thought out on every stance: (1) Exposure to rock or leader fall. If there is any choice, position yourself to one side of the line of ascent, lest a dislodged rock or the leader land on you and put you out of commission. (2) Direction of rope going to the leader. Pick a position from which the rope runs as directly as possible to the proposed line of ascent. This facilitates rope handling, for you can see what is going on. More important, it allows you to brace your legs against the force of a potential fall. (3) Direction of possible leader fall. This determines which will be the holding hand, as body friction must come between the holding hand and a fall. If the fall would be to your right, the right hand should guide the rope and the left hand do the actual holding, and vice versa. The route may change direction so the holding hand and the rope have to be switched to your other side, or the belay position moved; signals must be exchanged to assure that the leader is in a safe spot when such a change is made. (4) Belayer's comfort. This is the last among the considerations, but a sitting belay is easiest for a beginner and the most comfortable. Excellent belays can be given when necessary from a standing or crouching position, with the rope under the buttocks when the pull is from above, somewhat as in Figure 15; and over the hips when the pull is from below, similar to Figure 7.

Anchoring the Belayer

When the belay spot is selected, and in conjunction with determining the best position, the second should tie himself on well. He should take into account that the force of a fall may be sideways, downward, or upward (straight up or more often at a slant), according to the route and rock formation. He should be anchored so that he will be held in place regardless of the direction of the fall. Sometimes one or more pitons must be driven for anchors. Chocks can be used at times when you become an expert at placement; two or more are needed to cover all possible directions of pull. Attach yourself snugly to the anchor point with a carabiner in a sling, or with a small figure eight loop tied in a bight of the rope. Figure 15 shows a belay anchor. Do not un-anchor until the leader signals from above that he is ready for you to climb.

Holding Leader Falls

It is up to the leader to place protection so he cannot take a longer fall than his belayer can be expected to hold. But it is up to the belayer to stop, or try to stop, a fall quickly and no matter what.

In a sitting belay (the most common position), the rope usually runs around the belayer's hips *below* his anchor rope (as in Figure 7). It is a good position if protection has not yet been placed. It is also the best position if an anchor fails. It also minimizes the possibility of the rope riding up around the waist. When protection is in soundly, the belay rope may at times be placed under the belayer's buttocks (Figure 15), depending on the particular stance; this position is especially sound if the rope to the climber goes up at a sharp angle. To prevent any chance of the rope getting away from the belayer during a fall, he should clip it into a carabiner on the harness, on the braking side.

A leader fall is not necessarily hard to hold. There is much variation due to factors such as length of fall, soundness of protection, rope friction, and friction of the person falling. But don't *count* on the fall being easy to hold. If a fall occurs, grasp the rope as quickly and tightly as you can with both hands; simultaneously, advance your belay hand in front of the body to provide more friction, and brace your legs and your whole body for the shock. When that weight hits, hang on with all you've got! Modern nylon and perlon climbing ropes are very strong, and have sufficient elasticity to help greatly in absorbing the shock. If the fall is very severe, the rope will be yanked through your hands. But *hold on;* you can almost always brake it to a stop. A long fall can cause the rope to burn your hands (the reason some climbers wear leather gloves for belaying).

Several alternatives to traditional belaying techniques have been developed in the last few years. The use of belay plates—new pieces of hardware—lessens the chance of an injury. These devices are of special value to leaders. The force of a fall is absorbed

LEADER FALL

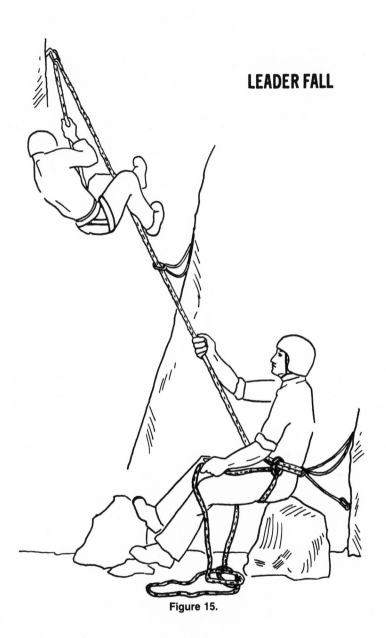

Figure 15.

almost automatically because any pull on the rope causes the belay plate to clamp around the rope. This system can also be used as an effective emergency lowering device if a climber cannot continue because of injury or for other reasons. Though body belays are adequate for the beginner, a belay plate is worth considering. Just make sure an experienced person demonstrates its operation—such devices are *extremely* dangerous if used improperly.

Belay plates have several important disadvantages. The rather sharp static bend in the rope (unlike the effect of a body belay) may damage or break the rope during a severe fall. The rope pays out slowly, which is bad when a climber could otherwise move swiftly. And it requires some time to engage and disengage.

Other Duties of the Second Man

Be sure the rope runs smoothly up to the leader, as a jerk can unbalance him in a delicate spot. Keep the rope in a loose pile (so it is less apt to tangle than if it is laid in a coil as it is taken in). While paying it out, allow a little slack between you and the leader so if he moves suddenly he won't be brought up short. Watch the rope carefully, and use your "feeling" hand to keep at least several feet free of tangles. If one hand is insufficient, or if you cannot undo it fast enough, ask the leader to stop while you unsnarl it. If the leader asks for tension, keep the rope tight until he calls "Slack!"

Notify the leader as to the approximate amount of rope left when there is about half remaining. This is easy if the middle of the rope is marked, as it should be. This gives the leader a clue as to when he has to find a belay spot. Thereafter call loudly, "Thirty" (or "Three-Oh"), "Twenty," "Ten," or whatever. Be emphatic if you get down to five. Occasionally a leader who has almost or just reached a belay stance with no rope to spare will ask you to unanchor or move a bit to give him a few feet more (do so with caution). The second man, of course, if he is also last, removes all the hardware and usually carries the pack.

Special Problems of the Middle Man

If there is a third on the rope, the second man is especially busy. He alternately belays leader and third man. He has to keep the two ropes separated, sometimes a puzzle if all three climbers are crammed onto one skimpy spot. (The others should help when possible.) The middle man has the same rope drag as the leader. When he comes to a carabiner, he takes the rope out of it, and clips the rope behind him into the same carabiner, running in the same direction. This gives the third man a fairly direct upper belay when the route changes direction, and provides needed protection on traverses. If friction is excessive, or if the leader needs the protective devices for re-use, the second may remove those not essential to the third's protection.

DESCENDING MULTI-PITCH CLIMBS

"What goes up must come down" applies to a tired and happy climbing party on top of cliff, peak, or spire. There are several modes of descent; not all are possible for every climb.

Walking Down

Usually the easiest and fastest, if trail or easy terrain take you where you want to go.

Climbing Down

Direct and quick on moderately easy climbs, either by the ascent route or by a different and easier *known* route (descent by unknown climbing routes frequently leads to trouble). Also, down climbing on purpose is a good way to gain experience before it is forced upon you. Climbing down is often harder than going up the same rocks; gravity is with you, but your anatomy is not so well suited to it—it is hard to see the holds and the route. Face outwards as long as you can; when necessary, turn sideways; and at steep places where you must face the cliffs to use the holds, combine feeling with your feet and occasional inspections. In down climbing, the leader goes last to protect the party. His second should place protection *below* difficult moves.

Rappelling

Often the chosen method of descent. It is easy and fun on cliffs fairly free of loose rock, and comparatively fast if the party is small and down climbing would be difficult. However, before you rappel on a multi-pitch climb, learn the technique with an upper belay—and learn it well! Rappelling is often more hazardous than the ascent.

Protection on Rappels. Under normal conditions, belayed rappels are uncommon for several reasons. There may be no spare rope; the process can be awkward and time-consuming; and a belay from below is of little use to the last man down. If loose rocks on the rappel route or other conditions make protection advisable while rappelling, a chest loop with a prussik knot fastened to the rappel rope can be used. The prussik is kept loose and unweighted, and the upper hand slides it down the rope.

Be sure that the prussik knot is well within reach when the prussik sling is fully extended, and that the clothing does not catch in the rappel rope whether or not a prussik is used. Deaths have occurred from both of these causes.

Take care while rappelling not to strain the rappel point or to knock down rocks with feet or rope; avoid long leaps (sometimes seen on practice cliffs and in movies). At the end of the rappel, each person should step to one side of the rope, and anchor if the position is insecure; remember you are unbelayed.

Rappel Points. The rappel must be fixed on an absolutely sound point in such a way that it cannot come off. Most rappel fatalities have occurred when the sling cut or broke or came off the point. Slings are advised for all rappel points, to protect the rappel rope and to lessen the friction when the rope is being pulled down. Stout trees or bushes provide excellent rappel points. Sound chock stones, protruding blocks, and flakes also are good. When a suitable natural feature is lacking, a dependable chock or piton can be used; more often two or three are spaced to divide the strain and back each other up. Several safe rappel points are shown in

Figure 16. If you cannot find a safe rappel point, you must climb down (or up) till you come to one.

The rappel must be rigged so the rope can be retrieved by pulling one end from below. Jamming or excessive friction is common if the rope is placed directly around the rappel point. The connecting link between rappel point and doubled rope is usually a strong sling long enough to hang free of obstructions. The sling may have to be untied or used double around a tree or behind a chock stone. Often the loop can just be dropped over a point or flake. Make sure it will stay there with a downward and somewhat sideways pull. If the sling has to go over sharp edges, pad it with paper, rags (your shirttail?) or whatever you have. *Never* trust an old sling found in place on the rock; it can look new yet be frail with old age or friction. Don't trust even your own slings too far; if in doubt of their adequacy, rig double for extra strength. Only in real desperation are carabiners used for setting rappels since they cannot be regained.

Rappel Rope. The rappel is usually made on the doubled climbing rope. If two ropes are available, they are usually tied together. If you are using only one climbing rope but plan on long rappels, take an auxiliary rope of about ⅜-inch diameter (9mm). Tying together two ropes of unequal diameter for a rappel must be done with extra care (see Flemish bend, Figure 3).

There is a great danger if two different types of rope are tied together; for example, a goldline with a perlon. Because the different kinds of rope may stretch at a different rate when loaded, they will tend to slide back and forth during a rappel. This is not a problem if one uses a small one-inch diameter rappel ring or a carabiner. But if the rappel line is threaded through a nylon sling, the rope could burn through the sling. This fact is often overlooked and has led to needless injuries.

When the sling is ready (or before, if it had to be untied and retied), one end of the rappel rope is put through the loop; the approximate middle of the rope bears on the sling, but to save wear on one spot don't use the exact center every time. Coil the ends separately, and throw them down the cliff one at a time, making sure someone holds the rope. Several tries are sometimes necessary to get the ends well down, especially with a light line. Some climbers throw each half down in two parts: first the coiled

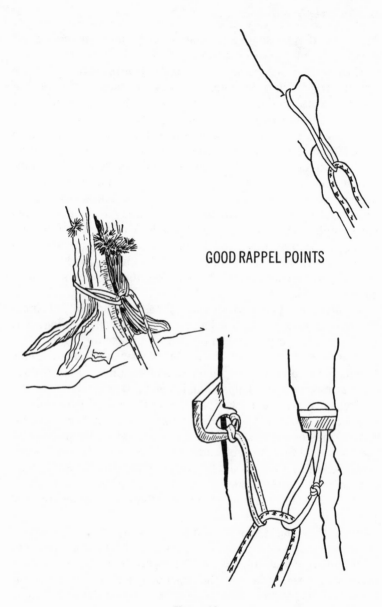

GOOD RAPPEL POINTS

Figure 16.

upper part and then the coiled end part. If the rope will not go down well, the first man to rappel must untangle it as he goes.

If the length of the rappel is unknown or the route of descent cannot be seen from above, tie the ends of the rappel rope together with an overhand knot. This can protect the first person down, by preventing him from sliding off the end of the rope should he miss the ledge.

Rappelling Methods. Opinions vary, but the best method of rappelling appears to be that using a seat harness and a figure-eight descender. However, sometimes one must use a simple body rappel, or may have only carabiners and a seat harness and slings.

One technique is the sling rappel. Tuck in all loose clothing and long hair that could otherwise get caught in the ropes. A sling four or five feet in circumference is twisted once, forming a figure eight with the knot at one side. Place each foot in one loop of the figure eight, and holding it in the center where the two sides cross, pull it up to your crotch (Figure 17). The sling should be of the right size so the two sides cross a few inches above the crotch. Holding the crossed portion in front of you, put three carabiners over it side by side (safer than one, and easier on the rope).

Pass the doubled rappel rope through the three carabiners (Figure 17), and turn the middle one so the gates face in alternating directions. From the carabiners (instead of from the hip as in the body rappel), the rope goes over one shoulder and is grasped below in the opposite hand, as shown in Figure 17. Rappelling then proceeds exactly as in the body rappel. Additional padding may be required at the shoulder if you are lightly dressed. In this type of rappel, if two ropes of unequal lengths must be tied together, remember that it is necessary to stop on a ledge when you reach the knot (or before) to pass it by the carabiners.

There are several new and widely practiced rappel friction systems. Figure-eight descenders are widely used. The Yosemite carabiner-brake rappel employs *six* carabiners: two clipped into the belay seat, two clipped into the first two carabiners, and two more set across after the rope is looped through the third and fourth carabiners. The loop runs over the solid sides of the last two carabiners creating the required friction. Care must be taken that the carabiners open from alternating sides: bottom-top, left-right, left-right, respectively.

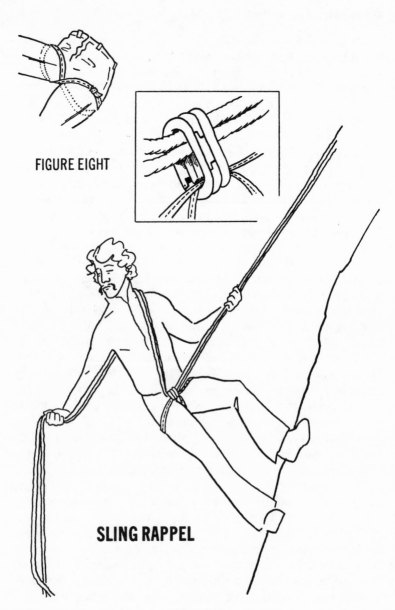

FIGURE EIGHT

SLING RAPPEL

Figure 17.

The point of these new methods is to increase comfort and safety. It is important to learn the use of this hardware with the help of an expert!

Roping Down. Descending a known route is desirable for a somewhat inexperienced party, as it helps the climber to be sure that the rope will reach from one rappel point to the next (often difficult or impossible to gauge from above). Be absolutely sure you are in the rope correctly. This can be confusing when you start the rappel from a particularly awkward position or from above the rappel point, but there is no room for error.

The most experienced climber usually goes down first to straighten the ropes and select the next rappel point. While one person rappels, the others should closely watch the rappel point and sling so they can give warning or take action if any weakness appears. When off rappel, the first man down tests the rope to make sure it can be retrieved; if it jams, the climbers above must rearrange it. The second most experienced comes down last.

The exact route of ascent is usually not followed on rappels because you tend to hang right below the rappel point, and better going on smooth sound rock can often be found by walking yourself to one side or the other. In going past an overhang, give a little push or jump when your upper hand comes to the lip, and descend a few inches while the hand is away from the rock. When you first hang free, you may pendulum a bit to one side or the other; you also tend to spin gently in the air on free rappels. Descend slowly to prevent rope burn, and don't let go!

Pulling Down the Rope. The last man down may keep a finger of the upper hand between the two sections of the rope to be sure they aren't twisted around each other; a glove protects the finger, but isn't really needed. When the entire party is down, untwist the two lengths if they still need it. Reclaim the rope by hauling on the end that has the knot below the sling (keep track of this). If there is no knot, pull whichever end comes easiest. A smooth, steady, rather fast pull is the surest way to get the rope down. Two people can pull alternately to keep it moving. When the rope starts to fall, duck! Occasionally the rope jams, and no amount of throwing, pulling and jerking in all possible directions will loosen it. Then someone has to climb up as far as necessary to free it, or as far as he can with or without a belay. Do not trust

Figure 18. Leaning back on a rappel.

the jammed rope for a handhold, as it can come unstuck at any time. In the rare instances when you cannot safely free it, cut off what you can salvage.

ROCK CLIMBING PLACES AND PRECAUTIONS

As stands to reason, rock climbing is most popular in areas where the accessible rock is beautifully adapted to the sport—Yosemite-type granite, for instance. In much-climbed areas, most routes are well established and have names (descriptive, gruesome, whimsical, or humorous). In non-mountainous areas there may be bluffs, palisades, cliffs, ravines, boulders, quarries, and road cuts (the last two usually loose), where you can sharpen your techniques and have fun. Bouldering has in itself become a rock climbing specialty.

With or without good climbing nearby, you may yearn to travel to other places, usually ones you have heard about, read about, or seen pictured—popular or possibly untouched. With techniques and equipment to suit the place, you will find that every area has its own appeal.

Extra care is expedient on unfamiliar or unclimbed routes when you are a long way from help, and the weather perhaps adverse. The climber functions less efficiently in extremes of heat, wind, and cold. Sudden changes in weather can transform conditions from good to bad almost instantaneously. Wet or snowy rocks are infinitely more difficult and dangerous than dry ones.

Weather may force a retreat. Other reasons for giving up a climb include illness, incompetence, fright, unwillingness or injury in the party, unexpected route difficulties, shortage of equipment, and an ''off day'' for the leader. The most common reason for retreat is lack of time to finish before dark. In deciding whether to go on or go back, remember that it may be quicker and safer to finish the climb if the top is closer than the bottom, if the climbing ahead is known to be easier than below, *and* if there is a fast, safe way down. Roped climbing and rappelling in the dark are hazardous. If night overtakes you on the cliffs, it is usually best to tie on in as good a place as you can find and stay put until daylight. When setting out next morning, compensate for the long hard night by using extra care.

Don't mess up the cliffs by leaving hardware or litter. A gum paper or juice can may seem insignificant when dropped—but will be offensive to the next fellow that comes across it, when he thought he was in the privacy and isolation of remote cliffs. Pick something up and carry it out instead; improve your unique world.

When you become adept at all this, you will no longer be a beginner. You may well be on the way to becoming an expert rock climber. And sooner or later, you may start to think of rock climbing as only one branch of the complex sport of mountaineering, which has other types of terrain to offer.

4

Equipment and Techniques for Snow Climbing

AS IS readily deduced from inspecting mountains with an eye to climbing them, some routes are all rock, others all snow and ice, and many a combination. A safe ascent of a route involving snow and ice requires familiarity with, and respect for, the substance.

SAFE CLIMBING ON SNOW AND ICE

An elementary knowledge of proper equipment, clothing, and techniques would avert many or most of the accidents that occur on snow and ice slopes. Such slopes often look deceptively easy to the uninformed. A person familiar with rock climbing has a head start in snow work, though there is no reason other than geographical chance or personal preference for taking up one before the other. Some of the techniques are very similar. As in rock climbing, snow and ice techniques are best learned through instruction and practice with able and experienced individuals or clubs, or in qualified courses or schools. Reading is helpful as background and reference, but is no substitute for workouts under skilled instructors. Beginners should start their practice on snow, preferably having a frozen texture. Except for occasional references to advanced ice work, this is the limited meaning of "snow and ice" as used in this chapter.

EQUIPMENT FOR SNOW AND ICE CLIMBING

For snow and ice, you *must* have adequate clothing and gear. Consult local climbers for advice. If you wish to try out equipment before buying, rent it from a mountaineering shop, borrow, or use equipment provided by a commercial climbing school or guide service.

Ice Axe

A special-purpose tool exquisitely designed for safeguarding and assisting the climber on snow and ice. The axe, illustrated in Figure 19, has a shaft that is oval in cross-section, and is usually between twenty-six and thirty-five inches long for all-around use (shorter for really steep ice climbs). Modern shafts are generally aluminum; some are composite aluminum-graphite-fiberglass. At one end of the shaft is a steel spike; at the other end is a head, usually between eleven and twelve inches long.

One end of the head is a blade or adze, either flat or curved; the other end is a sharp pick. The newest design is a "drooped" pick with a sharp chisel point (Figure 19), particularly good for step-cutting in ice. Some picks and ice hammers have interchangeable blades for different purposes.

The pick's chisel point should be slanted so that the top edge is slightly *closer* to the axis of the shaft than is the bottom edge as shown in Figure 19.

Most axes have a wrist loop of webbing attached to the shaft with a glide ring. A metal stop keeps the glide ring from sliding off. The carabiner hole in the head is for convenience in carrying the axe while rock climbing, or for rigging a long wrist loop as many prefer—it is *not* for belaying.

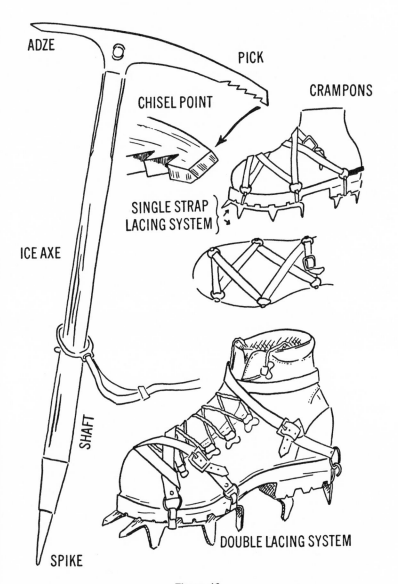

ADZE

PICK

CHISEL POINT

CRAMPONS

SINGLE STRAP
LACING SYSTEM

ICE AXE

SHAFT

DOUBLE LACING SYSTEM

SPIKE

Figure 19.

Despite differences in style, details, and prices, any well-chosen axe gives good service. Select one of sturdy workmanlike construction. Many shafts are partially coated for better grip and insulation. As to length (a moot point among climbers), for beginning work select an axe that feels comfortable in the hand as a staff. The trend is toward somewhat short axes, but for the novice, a *very* short one (often used on steep ice by experienced climbers) will be awkward as a staff and for step-cutting, and inefficient for self-arrests.

Proper care will keep the axe in good condition. The spike and pick of all axes should be kept sharp with a file. Check the wrist loop occasionally for wear, and replace when required. Store your axe in a dry place.

Boots

Important to protect the feet from cold, wet, and battering, and to give good traction. One style is shown in Figure 19. The sole has heavy rubber lugs, for both insulation and good footing on most terrain. The best lacing arrangement consists of rings near the instep and hooks above. Use nylon laces.

The boots should fit over one pair of thin nylon socks next to the feet, plus two pairs of wool socks. If low temperatures and/or long snow/glacier climbs are expected, provide room for more or thicker socks. You must have room to wiggle your toes, to avoid frostbite and other discomforts. Boots should have hard box toes to protect the feet when kicking steps and wearing crampons. Waterproof construction is essential: the fewer seams the better; look for a water welt; and the tongue should be sewn at least partway up, maybe clear to the top. Be sure the boot opens wide, so you can get it on when it is frozen stiff. Good boots are costly, but serve better and last much longer than cheap ones.

Your boots must be cared for to maintain their waterproof properties and shape, and to preserve the leather. After use, clean them well (wash if need be), and let them dry slowly; use a boot tree, or stuff them tightly with crumpled newspaper (change it frequently). Treat the leather with a liquid silicone preparation, especially all seams. Then rub in a coat of *wax*-based waterproofing. Warm the boots before applying it. Hot sun is best, but if there isn't any, a hot air register will do. If you must, use the oven—but with caution, as roasting ruins boots. Warm the oven *slightly,* and *turn it off* before putting the boots in. Set them on a thick pad of newspapers topped with aluminum foil. Keep your boots in good repair, and store them clean and waxed in an airy place. Mountaineering boots (and rock shoes) are often resoled, but this should be done only by a specialist in this type of repair.

And be sure to break your boots in gradually on short trips! You and your feet will suffer if you wear brand-new boots on a long jaunt.

Some manufacturers are producing "high tech" plastic boots which are lighter, warmer, and do not require the same water-proofing maintenance. Yet they are also more expensive. And some climbers report discomfort.

Crampons

A fundamental piece of snow and ice gear, though not used under all conditions. As shown in Figure 19, they are steel alloy assemblages of sharp metal spikes on a usually hinged framework that permits some flexibility. They are strapped to the boot; and in walking, the points bite into snow and ice. Modern crampons usually have twelve points, with two of the points sticking out in front to kick into steep slopes. Four-point instep crampons are not adequate. Rigid crampons are worn with rigid-soled boots for advanced ice work.

Boots and crampons must work as a solid unit; hence a good fit is essential. Choose your boots first. Have them on your feet when buying or renting crampons. Crampons have a right and left, like shoes. Some are adjustable—these cost more, but are usable longer as boots usually wear out first.

Crampons are held in place partly by the tight fit, and largely by a harness. The two most common types of harnesses are the double-strap, the easiest to adjust; and the single-strap. Both kinds are usually of neoprene-coated nylon, and are laced through the rings or hooks of the framework as shown in Figure 19. Some crampons have a piece of metal that goes around the boot heel; if not, it may be necessary to cross the strap behind the boot. The straps must be cinched up tight—but don't cut off the cir-

culation across your instep. The buckles go on the outside of the
foot, and the strap end is tucked in so it doesn't drag. Understand
the method of attachment perfectly, so you can apply it quickly
on the snow, in freezing weather, and even in the dark.

Keep crampons free of rust. File the points sharp when they
become dulled. Check the straps occasionally for signs of wear.

Rope

Essential in ice work, but the beginner should not be expected
to supply one while learning. An all-purpose 10.5 or 11mm perlon
(or a 7/16-inch laid nylon) rope, 120 to 150 feet long, is suitable for
a party of three, the preferred number on snow and glaciers. A
rope that becomes soaked or even superficially wet should receive
special attention at the end of the climbing day. Uncoil it, and
dry it under natural conditions (*not* near a campfire). Remove any
kinks both before and after drying. Chemically treated ropes increase resistance to abrasion and minimize water absorption.

Ice Screws and Pitons; Snow Flukes

Employed primarily by advanced climbers for protection or aid
on difficult ice climbs. Intermediate climbers may want a few
along for practice, for protection on unexpectedly steep or icy
slopes, or for emergency anchors. Keep in mind that ice pitons
and screws do not usually hold well in unfrozen snow or soft ice;
nor will they as a rule withstand as much strain as protection in
rock. If possible use nuts or pitons in sound rock bordering snow
slopes for superior protection.

Ice pitons and screws (Figure 20) are generally between six and
twelve inches long, and have large eyes. All have threads. Some
are hammered in; others are screwed in. Climbers generally call
the whole lot "screws." Be sure you know which type you have.
All appear to work well in freezing temperatures, as the ice melts
when they are driven, and they freeze in place. Some are better
than others for the warm summer weather usually encountered
on easy snow climbs. The best screws for all-around conditions
are hollow tubular screws.

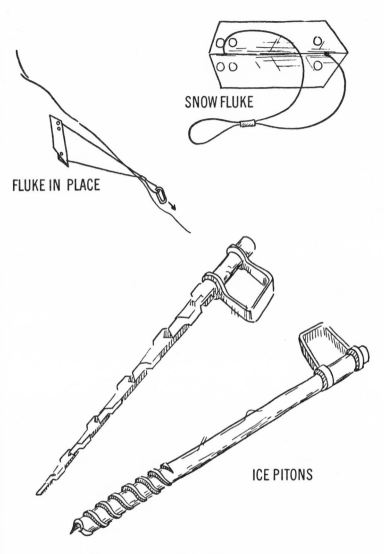

SNOW FLUKE

FLUKE IN PLACE

ICE PITONS

Figure 20.

Clear away loose surface ice or snow and start a hole with the axe pick. Insert the screw at an angle slightly uphill from the perpendicular to the line of potential pull. Tubular screws are started by hammering; use a piton hammer (advanced ice climbers have special alpine hammers with picks). Screw in screw types with another piton or the axe pick for a lever. Some types are hammered in and screwed out. Place ice screws clear to the eye. In removing, bend them as little as possible. The tubular ones may have retained a core of ice that must be removed before re-use; do it with a thin piton, a wire, or whatever will work.

Snow flukes (deadmen) are used as protective devices and belay anchors. These are metal plates, flat angled, fitted with nylon or wire slings (Figure 20). Bury them in the snow or drive them in at about forty-five degrees uphill from the line of pull, with the open side of the angle toward the slope. A pull on the wire should drive the fluke in deeper. Dig a narrow trench for the cables or slings so the fluke will not jerk outward. The larger flukes hold best in soft snow. Use slings and carabiners on snow as on rock.

CLOTHING FOR SNOW AND ICE CONDITIONS

Adequate clothing must be available for protection against cold, wet, wind, and sun. All such conditions are intensified on snow. If climbers are not appropriately dressed, the results may be serious or fatal, as discussed in Chapter 6.

Underwear

Long underwear is essential unless the outer pants are woolen, and may be needed even then. Wool is the traditional and proven fiber that continues to feel warm and to insulate even when wet. New synthetic materials, or combinations of wool and synthetics, are being developed and tried out under various conditions. "Fishnet" and some synthetic underwear are for use under outer clothing to allow perspiration to escape.

Pants

These should be hard-weave wool and/or nylon that does not collect snow. Be sure trousers or knickers are loose enough for freedom of movement. Long pants should taper toward the feet, and be held down by elastic under the instep, or tied around the ankle with a drawstring, unless gaiters are worn.

Socks

All-wool socks are mandatory, except for a little nylon reinforcing (and maybe a thin nylon pair to spare the skin from friction). Wear at least two heavy pairs. With knickers, one pair should reach to the knees or above.

Gaiters

Keep snow out of boot tops. Short ones are four to eight inches high, with elastic at top and bottom; long gaiters extend to just below the knee (Figure 23). Either type may have zippers that allow the gaiter to be put on or taken off over the boots; but ice-clogged zippers are no joy. Big heavy nylon zippers, preferably coil type, are least troublesome but are still a pain to do up in the cold. This trouble can be mitigated by getting gaiters that lace. Instep cords or straps go under the boots and hold the gaiters down firmly; fasten only on snow—rocks may cut them.

Shirts, Sweaters, Jackets

Several lightweight layers permit adaptation to temperature changes. The bottom layer is often a cotton shirt that is cool but protects against sunburn. Other shirts and sweaters should be woolen. Down jackets are very warm, very expensive, and not needed for a beginner's type of trip. They are for extreme cold. Down is also light and compressible. Its main drawback is the loss of insulating power when wet. Spun synthetic filament is used in wet areas as a down substitute; apparently it absorbs little water and remains fluffy enough to insulate even when soaked. Synthetics are also extremely thin and lightweight.

Parka and Poncho

A generously cut, windproof, water-repellent parka, with a roomy hood and many pockets, is a necessity as an outer garment. Choose a tight-weave poplin of cotton, nylon, or both. The weave and chemical treatments both provide water repellency. An old parka that leaks can be treated to restore a degree of water resistance. "Water-repellent" is far from waterproof, however; it is useful to have a lightweight plastic poncho or jacket along.

Hat, Cap, Mittens

Helmets and hard hats are seen increasingly on ice and snow work. For beginning practice trips, it is sufficient to wear a hat, preferably of felt, with a brim which protects in sun, rain, and snowfall. A woolen cap should be available—much heat is lost through the head. Woolen mittens (warmer than finger gloves) should be carried. Extra mittens, plus water-repellent nylon or canvas "covers," should be taken on all trips longer than a few hours.

Sun Protection

The effects of the sun cause acute problems on snow because of reflection, especially at high elevations and in spring and summer, at times even with an overcast sky. Goggles or dark glasses are *essential*. A good sunburn cream can be found in mountaineering shops or pharmacies (most popular beach types let you fry). Some recently developed types block out harmful rays completely. These are helpful for those with sun-sensitive skins. Special preparations are made for lips. Apply the goo to areas affected by reflection, and areas not normally a problem; and *re-apply* often.

WHERE TO LEARN

As a neophyte suitably outfitted, you are better off than an unequipped visitor to the snow slopes. But you must learn and practice the proper handling of your equipment under able tutelage.

Those giving instruction should select a safe practice slope, its steepness correlated with the snow texture. It should have a safe runout, without rocks, trees, or precipices at the bottom. Here you can practice the techniques basic to safe snow and ice work.

ICE AXE TECHNIQUES

Aside from proper boots, the ice axe is the *sine qua non* of snow and ice climbing. It is in constant use whether or not rope and crampons are needed. The major functions of the axe's parts are: (1) Spike: used like the bottom end of a cane in walking, or to drive into the snow for stability. (2) Adze or blade: for cutting steps in hard snow. (3) Pick: for cutting steps in ice, for self-arrests, or to jam into steep slopes so the shaft can be used for a handhold. (4) Shaft: to use as a staff, and as a belay point.

The many uses of the axe are mastered with practice. Always its three sharp points must be recognized as dangerous and treated circumspectly.

Transporting and Carrying the Ice Axe

While not in use, the axe is often equipped with a rubber guard over the spike, and a leather or rubber sheath for the head. To carry the axe when walking, hold the shaft at the balance point and carry it parallel with the ground, point forward and pick down. It may also be tucked under one arm in this position. When the axe is used as a walking stick, the head provides comfortable support for the hand.

Wrist Loop

Used where the axe is needed for safety, yet would be lost if dropped. The loop is primarily a safeguard against dropping the axe in a careless moment, *not* a substitute for keeping a tight grip on the axe in use. Some climbers disapprove of wrist loops, one reason being that a dropped axe, flailing from the wrist in a fall, can cause serious injury. But it is far worse to lose your axe, hence your chance to self-arrest!

Walking Up Easy Slopes

Walking up a practice slope is the beginning of learning to climb steep snow. Start straight up the slope, kicking your toes into the snow. Make footsteps fairly close together, to conserve energy and accommodate others who may use the steps. Use the axe as a staff, with the pick outwards. In this position the axe is ready for instantaneous use for a self-arrest. When the angle steepens, start to make switchbacks. Hold the axe in the uphill hand, changing it from hand to hand at the turns; if you feel insecure, stop to make the change before turning. Plant each foot firmly, and stamp or kick footsteps if necessary. Dropping your weight over the forward foot at each step minimizes the need to kick. Keep your weight directly over your feet for balance; if you lean into the slope, your feet tend to skid out from under you. When several people ascend together, they should all use the same footsteps; but each should stay a little behind the one in front.

Self-Arrests

A major function of the axe is to slow down or stop your slide after a fall. It is a vital skill, whether you are roped or unroped. It should be learned on safe slopes and soft snow. Roll down your sleeves and put on mittens. Hold the axe in the arrest position as follows: The axe head is held near your shoulder, with fingers over the head and thumb under the adze. The pick points forward so it will dig into the snow when you fall on the axe. The shaft slants diagonally downward across your chest, and your other hand grasps it near the spike, holding the tip-end near your hip.

Next, lie facedown in the snow, with the axe under you, as shown in Figure 21. Let yourself slide downhill feet first. Arch your back slightly to press the pick into the snow under your shoulder—most of the body weight is centered over the pick. The friction of pick in snow should gradually stop your fall. Repeat on increasingly steep or fast slopes. On fast crusty snow, start the pressure at once, but drive the pick in gradually lest the axe be ripped out of your hands. Don't let the spike catch, or it will flip you. As the slide becomes faster, spread your legs for balance and brake with your boot toes. In soft snow dig in your knees and elbows.

Since a real fall is not always in a conveniently perfect arrest position, practice getting into that position from various awkward starts. Start the slide on your back; curl your body a bit and roll over quickly toward the side on which you are holding the axe head. Next try sliding down headfirst, on your stomach; dig in the pick, and to get your legs downhill swing them around the pivot formed by the pick. Next start down on your back headfirst; roll onto your stomach and quickly pivot into a feetfirst position. Your instructor may suggest variations. Practice until you can arrest yourself automatically without thought.

When you start climbing potentially dangerous slopes, observe the gradient and surface of the snow, and the length and nature of the runout. The speed with which you start an arrest may determine whether it will succeed or fail.

ROPE TECHNIQUES FOR SNOW AND ICE CLIMBING

If self-arrests always worked, there would be no need of a rope. However, on slopes very soft, hard, steep, or with dangerous runouts, the climber cannot always stop himself soon enough, if at all. Hence, as on steep rocks, the roped team collaborates for mutual protection.

Roping Up

The preferred number of climbers on one rope on ice is three (two or three on snow). The amount of rope between climbers is shorter than on rock. If the available rope is too long, one climber ties to the end with the usual bowline, but leaves about two feet extra at the end. The unwanted portion of rope is wound over one shoulder and under the opposite arm; this coil is then secured with a bowline-on-a-coil tied with the rope end (Figure 1). This system permits easy lengthening of the rope if required. The middle man uses the figure eight loop (Figure 3).

SELF-ARREST

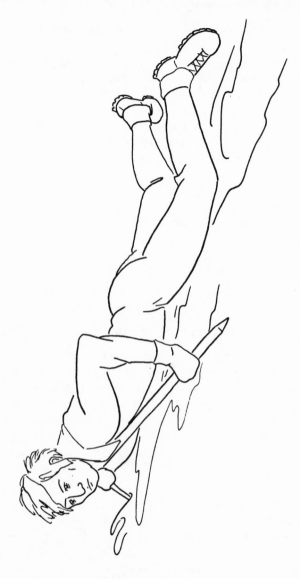

Figure 21.

BOOT-AXE BELAY

Figure 22.

Methods of Climbing

As in rock climbing, the best climber goes first as a rule, and the least experienced last or in the middle. There are two methods of progress, continuous and consecutive (both applied on rocks of ease or difficulty also).

Continuous Climbing. Used where a fall can probably be stopped though all are moving. The roped climbers walk at the same time, each adjusting his pace to the others'. When one stops, the others may have to wait for him. They should stay far enough apart so there is little or no slack in the rope between them. Each climber holds one or two coils of rope in his free hand, to help adjust his pace to the others and to allow a slight warning in case of a fall. (A beginner often feels he needs another hand.)

Consecutive Climbing. Used when the ascent is steeper, the snow icier, or the terrain dangerous—and where it would be hard to hold a fall without being set for it. One climber moves while the others belay him. The sequence of climbing is much like that of multi-pitch rock climbing.

Rope Handling

Moisture and temperature affect the rope on snow work. In cold dry weather on hard snow, the rope may stay dry even if dragged. If the snow is wet, the rope will get wet too. While climbing, hold it above the snow; hang your coil on the axe head when you stop instead of laying it in the snow; etc. The wetter the rope, the harder to handle because of increased weight and friction. Water is transferred to mittens and other clothing. Knots are harder to tie and untie. When the temperature drops, a wet rope freezes, becoming slippery, stiff, even covered with hoar frost.

BELAYING ON SNOW AND ICE

Establishing a sound belay is more difficult on snow than on rock. A sitting or standing hip belay is best and safest. It can be given as in rock work if the belayer is well braced in a depression or hole, against a rock, or on various stances manufactured with the axe. If no such belay spot exists, especially where slopes are moderate, use a boot-axe belay.

Boot-Axe Belay

This is another technique that is controversial, but useful on snow within its limitations. The ice axe and boot work together to establish a belay point quickly that can stop most moderate falls. To give the boot-axe belay: (1) Stand sideways to the slope, facing in the general direction of the climber. (2) Kick or cut two sound and ample steps, one uphill and slightly in front of the other. The downhill foot is braced in the lower footstep, leg straight. (3) On the uphill side of the upper footstep, drive the axe as far as possible down into the snow; clear to the head is best. The pick points uphill. (4) Plant the outside of the uphill boot firmly against the lower side of the axe shaft, at a right angle to the probable fall line. (5) The rope that comes from the climber should be passed over the toe of the boot; around the axe shaft; then downhill between the shaft and the instep. Figure 22 shows a belayer taking in rope in the boot-axe belay position. This belay feels awkward at first, but when it is fully understood, you can apply it very rapidly by jamming the axe into the snow in the proper relationship to the rope, and stamping your foot against the shaft, almost simultaneously. (6) For more friction in holding a fall, move the belay hand back between your legs, and uphill behind the boot heel, in the S-bend. (7) The uphill hand grasps the axe head, with your weight holding the axe down.

Belay Practice

Falls should be held for practice, as in rock climbing. To practice the boot-axe belay, first try it with a climber coming up from below. Your axe hand can be used to help take in rope; but in a fall return it instantly to the axe head. Never remove your downhill (belay) hand from the rope. Try increasingly severe falls. Belay the leader in the same position as is used for an upper belay, keeping the axe hand in its position and weight over the axe. Think out the probable direction of the fall. When the weight hits, the rope should run a little—easier on the axe (and the belayer).

Team Belays

On snow, no one person is completely responsible for holding a fall. The person falling should immediately go into a self-arrest, and call "Fall!" Others on the rope get into belay position fast if they are not already in it. If they are pulled off, they too go into a prompt self-arrest.

ASCENDING DIFFICULT SLOPES

As steeper slopes are climbed, on snow that is icier, or deeper, softer, and less stable, methods learned so far are applied with greater finesse. The axe becomes a sort of handhold when needed. In soft, unstable snow, the shaft is sunk deeply on the uphill side at each step. In precarious places, it is moved from one hole to the next while the climber is standing still. Where the snow is hard and icy, either spike or pick may be used on the uphill side for balance or a slight purchase. The axe is used also to feel and probe the snow for invisible ice or other textural changes. Where kicking footsteps becomes arduous or ineffective, the adze can be used to cut steps. To replace or augment step cutting, crampons may be used.

CRAMPON TECHNIQUES

Your first try at walking up a crusty snow slope with crampons is apt to be wildly successful! The points bite into the glittering white surface, and your footing seems secure beyond human possibility. But as with other equipment, crampons must be properly used.

Storage and Transport

The points are dangerous, and must be treated as such to prevent injuring yourself and others. They must also be protected to keep them sharp. Cover the points when out of use, and be careful when wearing them. At home or in the car, store them in a box. On the rucksack, use bought crampon protectors, or stick sections of rubber tubing on the points. They can also be lashed points-down on opposite sides of a styrofoam rectangle.

Learning to Walk on Crampons

You should have a frozen surface and gentle gradient to practice on. Lay the crampons on the snow, points down; straighten the harness; and shove your boots in place. Lash them on; adjustment is sometimes necessary after about the first five minutes, and occasionally thereafter.

Take each step with the crampon flat on the snow surface. This may require strength and flexibility of the ankles. Place the foot down firmly and precisely with each step, stamping as hard as necessary, or letting your body weight fall forward over the foot, to drive the points into the snow. Raise each foot high enough to prevent tripping on the points.

Cautions

One of the hazards in cramponing is the possibility of catching the points on the opposite leg. You can trip, or tear your clothes or your hide. Wear pants not too full in the legs, or confine them in gaiters. Knickers and long socks lessen but do not eliminate this hazard. Walk with your feet well apart, and don't toe in. Perfect your balance; if you do fall, remember that the points may puncture someone (maybe you). In making a self-arrest in crampons, *don't* brake with the toes; a crampon point catching in the snow may flip you, so keep your knees bent. In soft snow, balls of snow may form between the points; knock them loose periodically with a tap of the axe, or a kick with the side of one foot against the opposite boot.

Increasingly Difficult Slopes

Crampons are often used for convenience on hard snow that is flat, but their greatest value is on icy slopes that seem steep. Once put on for a climb, they are often worn all day long, needed or not, to save the trouble of removing and re-installing. On your early climbs you may not encounter really long, steep, icy slopes. But it is a somewhat relative matter; what takes all your skill and nerve during your first season may seem easy the next year. As the slopes become steeper and icier, be especially attentive to balance; both feet and body are positioned somewhat as in friction-climbing on rock. Climbers also may cut steps when wearing crampons. Enjoy your crampons, perfect your mastery of them, and learn to trust them on both the ascent and the descent.

DESCENDING SNOW AND ICE

The descent of a given slope is usually made in much the same manner and with the same equipment and protection as the ascent, under stable conditions. Even greater care is necessary; your momentum is already downward.

Climbing Down

If an ascent required careful climbing, the descent probably will also, though snow conditions may be better or worse. The party uses the footsteps of the ascent, if possible. The leader generally goes last in a roped party descending on steep, hard, or unstable snow. Snow that was soft on the ascent may have grown icy, or hard snow may have softened and be poorly consolidated. The first person down should improve the old steps, or cut or kick new ones. Climb down backwards if you must, both hands on the axe.

Walking Down

If snow is soft and gradient moderate, nothing more specialized than walking down is required. Even this should be done properly to save time and energy. Going straight down, let your weight come down on your heel at each step, to drive it into the snow. Take more deliberate care if the slope seems steep or the snow crumbly, and use your axe at one side as a staff. The party may be roped but move together. When snow and slope are easier, let each heel slide for a couple of feet in the "plunge step"—a rapid easy mode of walking down. Under ideal conditions, all can run down in their own courses, using the plunge step and holding axes in arrest position.

Glissading

Glissading is a fast and felicitous way to descend when texture and slope are just right; but potentially dangerous if you misjudge conditions. Practice on short slopes with safe runouts. The gradient must be fairly steep or the technique won't work. Build up gradually to longer faster glissades, but always look for a safe runout in case you lose control. It just isn't healthy to end a glissade in a rock pile or over a cliff.

Glissades are made sitting or standing (Figure 23). The sitting position is safest and easiest. To get ready, remove your crampons and stow them safely (*not* outside the rucksack with points at the ready); batten down your clothing; put on mittens. Hold the axe in arrest position. Sit down with legs out straight and heels off the snow. Take off. The spike of the axe can be used on either side as a rudder for slight changes of direction, or to slow you down a bit. A major change in course must be accomplished by stopping and traversing on foot to a new starting point. To stop, dig in your heels and your axe spike, or roll over in a self-arrest. On soft snow, pillows of it may form under your rear; hunch over them. Rough terrain or small rocks can be rather bruising. The most uncomfortable effect is getting wet. If staying dry is important, walk or make a standing glissade.

A standing glissade (Figure 23) is done with more style and aplomb, and is suited to steeper slopes when sufficient experience and judgment have been gained. It is more strenuous on the legs, and resembles skiing without skis. The axe is used on one side, for support and steering. Undertake your first standing glissades with caution, at first on short slopes to get the feel of it. Good judgment of snow conditions in relation to the incline, as well as skill at glissading under control, is required for all safe glissading.

Use your equipment until it seems to be part of you; work on

GLISSADING

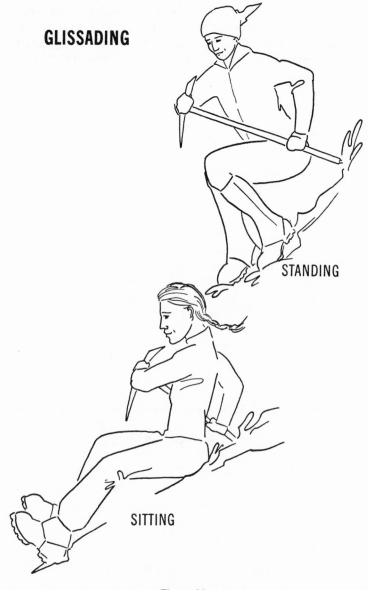

STANDING

SITTING

Figure 23.

basic techniques until they become automatic, both on practice slopes and on easy climbs. You are then ready to concentrate on the multitude of other factors that contribute to proficiency and judgment in ascents and descents on snow, ice, and glacier climbs— and perhaps to look forward to ascents on steep ice with all the specialized paraphernalia of modern ice work.

5

Snow, Ice, and Glacier Terrain

BESIDES technical skills, a growing knowledge of the complex environment encountered on snow and ice climbs is a necessary ingredient of safe mountain ascents. Such knowledge is gained bit by bit, over a period of many seasons, in many weathers, on diverse peaks. A theoretical acquaintance with the common conditions that you will encounter or should avoid will help you recognize and cope with them.

WHERE TO FIND SNOW AND ICE CLIMBING

The most obvious snow and ice climbing is on glacier peaks. However, the snow may be unrelated to the glaciers on a particular peak, or may exist on non-glacier peaks, where it is often found alternating with rock. Superficially, the same techniques are used on glacier or non-glacier snow work; actually, non-glacier snow work is much simpler. Excluding winter ascents, which are not for the inexperienced, such terrain is encountered either early in the season, or on the north sides of peaks, in shaded couloirs, and on other parts of mountains where snow has piled deep and has been protected from the sun. Such areas often provide snow and ice routes during the summer, long after the opportunities of early-season climbing have melted away, especially in years of heavy or late snowfall.

SNOW AND ICE CONDITIONS AND HAZARDS

Routes involving snow and ice may be sought out for several reasons. Perhaps you prefer it, or cannot avoid it, or find it easier than rock. There are many obvious differences from rock climbing and some that are less apparent.

Changes in Surface

Snow and ice are extremely variable. The surface changes with temperatures, elevation, exposure, weather, and season. It varies from year to year, from day to day, even from hour to hour. For instance, a particular couloir in the thaws of springtime may be a menacing avalanche of water, sloppy snow, and loose rocks pouring down from the walls above. Similar conditions can exist after a storm. In early summer the same gully may present an excellently consolidated surface. On hot days the snow is often crumbly and unstable. On a cold morning it may require crampons, but by afternoon be ideal for glissading. A surface of snow may change to ice at any step. There is often water ice at the head of the couloir. By autumn, the same gully may be almost dry or have melted down to old snow nearly as hard as ice. A new snowfall could mask conditions that exist just below the surface. Observation, calculation, and investigation will frequently be required before you decide on the route; sometimes you must choose a different route or even give up the climb.

Similar changes in texture are constantly occurring on snowfields and slopes. A firm surface of consolidated summer snow is ideal to walk on, far easier than talus if there is a choice. On very hard or icy snow, you will need crampons. Snow that has alternately thawed and melted over a long period of time forms surface pits known as sun cups, separated by ridges. Sun cups make good belay spots, and often make for safe walking even on quite steep slopes. As the season advances, the pits become more pronounced, and at times they become so deep, with such high ridges between, that much energy is expended climbing from one to another.

A phenomenon of no importance in climbing, but interesting since it is seldom seen by anyone but climbers, is red snow. This is "watermelon snow," named from the color and odor that suddenly bloom in each footstep or give a reddish cast to an entire snowfield. This effect is caused by certain algae (the most common is *Chlamydomonas nivalis*) which live in the snow, and develop red pigment during their resting stage in late summer.

Soft, wet, poorly consolidated snow, usually found between early- and mid-season climbing, may hold your weight at one step, yet allow your foot to plunge in deeply at the next. At best this is exhausting, and at worst unspeakable! Your leg can become so heavily embedded in snow that you have to free it with your axe. Snow may also conceal the existence of lakes or streams under the surface. You can usually hear running streams, but there is no such warning of lakes in flat areas. Suddenly your foot may be immersed in water below the surface. Try to get away from the soft area by changing course.

A similar situation arises when unbroken snow conceals rocks that lie close to the surface with hidden spaces melted around them; this is especially common close to other rocks that protrude from the surface, and in places where snow and talus meet. A big step or jump to visibly sound footing will avoid most of these hidden holes.

Many changes in texture can be guessed at according to temperatures and general snow conditions. Others, such as abrupt changes from snow to ice, can be determined by probing with the axe. Be constantly on the alert for altered conditions.

Melt Holes and Moats

Other conditions due to melt are the deep holes that form around rocks, and the moats at the base of cliffs. In these places, the snow either did not pack well in the first place, or melted faster than the rest because the darker object beside it absorbed more heat. Moats are often so huge that they are a real danger, especially if covered. Even if they are open, they may extend back under the snow much farther than is obvious. To a degree, it is wise to give protruding rocks a wide berth. The moats along the bottoms of cliffs may sometimes be taken advantage of, as they may provide easier and safer climbing than the adjacent snow.

Avalanches, Rockfalls, and Cornices

Slopes that are likely to avalanche should not be climbed, and must be crossed with extreme caution. Masses of avalanching snow may suffocate, crush, or simply bury you without a trace. But you have to recognize an avalanche slope to avoid it. Snow avalanches are, of course, much more common in winter and spring than in the latter part of the summer, the normal climbing season. In general, avoid gullies and steep, unbroken slopes that are covered with either deep snow (wet, dry, or windpacked), or by large amounts of melting snow. Extensive observation and experience should eventually provide a background knowledge of when and where slopes are stable enough to climb, and the time and route for a safe crossing. While gaining knowledge, avoid couloirs that look hazardous above or that present evidence of avalanche activity below (vertical grooves, ice and snow blocks, etc.). Ridges often provide safe alternate routes.

Less obvious, and lasting perhaps through the climbing season, is the possibility of spontaneous rockfall. The danger especially exists on rock faces, or in snow and ice gullies that lie between rock cliffs, during periods of heavy melting. The evidence of rockfall can be easily seen in gullies of snow and ice. Rocks and dirt may lie on the snow surface, either in the couloir proper or at its foot in a fan. Long vertical grooves in the snow are unmistakable marks of either avalanche or rockfall. These indications may be concealed by even a light snowfall, however, which at the same time adds to the danger. Some walls seem to discharge rocks at any time, others only when in the sun. The signs in the snow can suggest to you which part of the gully is safe to ascend and which part dangerous. A broad couloir is more apt to provide a safe route than a narrow one.

Cornices are another feature that should be avoided altogether by climbers of limited experience, and should be recognized and understood. They are overhangs of snow shaped almost like ocean waves, gradually built up as winter winds blow over the steep drop from the windward side of the crest. As an inexperienced climber you presumably would not climb beneath a cornice's overhanging side or try to cut your way through it. But you very well might arrive on a nice broad snow ridge from the easy side, without realizing that the flat area is, in part, hanging unsupported over nothingness on the steep side. By observing surrounding ridges, looking for a possible crack line, probing with your axe, and exercising caution, you can avoid getting out on the cornice beyond its probable line of fracture.

Temporary Snow and Ice Conditions

Conditions with which the climber must cope, even though they are not strictly snow and ice climbing, occur during or after sudden storms. The new snow tends to blow, melt, or fall off steep rocks, while lying inconveniently cold, wet, and slippery on handholds and footholds. Snow which has melted and then frozen, or rain which has frozen, may coat rocks with thin, almost invisible, glassy ice called verglas. Snow, either fresh or melting, may cause avalanches and rockfall in gullies and troughs, or hide the nature of what lies beneath the surface. Such conditions must be dealt with by increased safety measures both in use of equipment and in general attitude.

GLACIERS, WHAT AND WHERE

All of the problems, conditions, techniques, safeguards, equipment, and clothing that pertain to snow and ice work are also applicable to glacier climbing. Superficial conditions are much the same for both, but some additional conditions of vital importance to climbers are built right into glacier structure.

In simplified form, glaciers may be described as large masses of slowly moving ice that exist as permanent features of mountain architecture. They form and thrive in mountainous or other regions where weather, climate, exposure, elevation, and latitude combine, over long periods of time, to permit sizable accumulations of snow which become compressed into ice. Such an ice mass moves slowly downhill, melting at its lower margin and being renewed by fresh snow in its upper portions, with the seasons. The transition zone between snow and ice is called firn or névé.

The extent of glaciers varies enormously. One mountain may be mainly rock, with one small glacier and some snow chutes. Another may be covered almost completely by a vast network of glaciers, perhaps separated by rock ridges in their upper portions and flowing into each other in their lower reaches. There are limitless combinations. The surface of a glacier may look like a snowfield. It may be large or small, rough or quite smooth, sparkling with fresh snow or so covered with gravel and dirt that it is hard to believe ice lies underneath. The ice itself is seen late in the year when the snow on top has melted, in tumbled icefalls or at glacier snouts, or in the deep fissures of crevasses that form great cracks in the ice.

RELATION OF GLACIER MOTION TO CLIMBING

For climbers, the most vital thing about glaciers is the formation and endless change of crevasses and bergschrunds. As the ice moves over steep or uneven parts of its course, or is forced by the shape of its bed to change direction, splits and cracks form in the ice at or near the surface. These fissures may be mere notches (good for belays), narrow cracks you can jump over, or formidable dark caverns hundreds of feet deep. Some have shining ice walls or reveal many layers of old ice and dirt. You may hear water running in crevasses or see enormous icicles festooning their walls. They are sometimes gapingly obvious, and at other times covered securely or insecurely with snow. They are most prevalent at manifestly steep, convex, or irregular sections of the flow. A crevasse may be anywhere, however; and where there is one, there are often others roughly parallel to it. Where the glacier breaks away from the mountain at or near its upper end, an enormous crevasse or series of crevasses forms—this is called the bergschrund. The ever present danger of falling into a crevasse is the main difference between ordinary snow or ice climbing, and glacier travel.

Additional Effects of Glacier Motion

Other results of glacier motion are continuous and current processes—some important, some merely of interest. One by-product of glaciers is the finely ground silt, or "glacier flour," discharged in the melt water. This silt gives the beautiful opaque greens and blues to many high-mountain lakes, and the dense, milky (or dishwatery) appearance to streams originating in glaciers. A glacial river is difficult to ford because (among other reasons) you cannot see the bottom. People sometimes think twice before drinking water so full of grit, even though it is perfectly harmless and most of the particles soon settle when the water stands in a cup or pot.

HOW TO START GLACIER CLIMBING

A climber new to glacier travel—even if he has mastered the fundamentals of snow and ice—should not venture upon a glacier without experienced companions. Build up judgment by paying close attention to your intricate and changing environment, in the company of knowledgeable climbers. Learn how to plan glacier routes from a distance and close up, to avoid heavily crevassed areas. Heed details of technique that make you a safe member of the party, and take full advantage of the formal or informal instruction offered on your early glacier climbs.

When you have gained experience with such groups, and begin to go out on your own, start with routes reasonably familiar. Forego obvious and unnecessary complications such as icefalls, and unknown routes on unfamiliar peaks, until you have well-founded confidence in your capabilities developed on easier and better-known routes. And always practice established safety measures for glacier travel.

SAFETY MEASURES FOR GLACIER TRAVEL

Glacier travel is too varied and complicated for a list of arbitrary "rules," but necessary precautions that will greatly increase the likelihood of your staying (or getting) out of crevasses can be given as a guide.

(1) Wear or carry adequate clothing. Surface temperatures may be summery, but it is always wintertime inside a crevasse.

(2) Always rope up on glaciers, even on an easy or flat slope. Crevasses exist on flat portions of some glaciers, and in sections where they have been previously unknown.

(3) Three on a rope is the preferred number for glacier travel. Two or more ropes traveling together are safer than one.

(4) Always wear the wrist loop of your ice axe, which you must not lose.

(5) Before setting off across a glacier, attach three prussik slings to the rope and stow them in pockets or otherwise out of the way (not in your waist loop). The middle man should put one of the slings on the rope going to the man behind him. He might be held on either rope, and need a loop to stand in while adjusting the other slings. Make sure the foot stirrups are big enough to go on easily when you are wearing crampons.

(6) Tie a small loop in the rope a few feet from the waist loop, to anchor a fallen climber with the axe through the loop.

(7) Where ease of climbing permits, travel continuously, the rope fully extended between climbers, and each member of the rope prepared to give a belay instantly if one person disappears into a crevasse.

(8) You are not apt to fall into a wide-open crevasse. The danger lies in those hidden beneath a snow surface too weak to bear your weight. Such spots can sometimes be detected by a long trough of slightly depressed snow, or other textural changes. Each climber should probe the surface with his axe; it goes in more readily and deeply if a thin layer of snow over a hole has been reached. When you find one crevasse, suspect others nearby. If possible, walk at right angles to suspected crevasses, and avoid having the entire party over the same crevasse. If moving parallel to crevasses, the climbers should follow well-separated paths instead of the leader's footsteps.

(9) If someone falls into a crevasse in continuous climbing, the others on the rope must instantly drop into belay or arrest positions. Change to consecutive climbing with careful belays when the climbing becomes difficult or any but minor crevasse crossings are contemplated.

CROSSING CREVASSES

All crevasses deserve careful inspection, partly for reasons of their sheer sensational interest, but especially with a view to getting safely to the other side. Consider how serious a fall would be, and how difficult it would be to get out. Some are narrow and shallow, but have slick walls that converge so you could be wedged in. Some are water-filled. Others are so full of snow that a landing might be soft and harmless, but you also might fall right through the apparently solid snow. There may be broad ledges near the top or black depths the eye cannot measure. Some have gentle walls that appear easily climbable. Others may be undercut in a "bell" shape that is especially difficult to surmount.

Many crossings can (or must) be avoided, either by laying out a route that bypasses crevasses altogether or by detouring around the ends. A crevasse that is partly or largely snow-covered requires particularly close inspection, as the ends or edges may be unstable. "Bridges" of snow sometimes present the shortest or perhaps the only way to get across, but must be inspected carefully from every angle for thickness, stability, and surface cracks that might indicate weakness. When the crossing is to be attempted, set up belays well away from the edge. The leader should step with care and test with his axe. On the far side, he should make sure he is beyond the first crevasse but not above another when he sets up his belay. The second and subsequent persons should step gently in the leader's steps (unless he made a hole), and they too should probe. A bridge frozen solid in the morning may be ready to collapse by the return in the afternoon.

Bergschrunds present similar problems, but may be more trouble than other crevasse crossings, partly because they often cannot be avoided. Bergschrunds are often easy to cross early in the season when covered or clogged with snow, especially at one end. Or they may present almost insuperable difficulties late in the season, when the chasm is so vast that you must climb down into it and out again. This may be unusually difficult because of a much higher, overhanging upper lip. Sometimes it is better to give up the peak than make the bergschrund crossing twice. If you do get across, take pains not to fall into it from the steep slopes above.

GETTING OUT OF CREVASSES

With care (and luck), you have a good chance of never falling into a crevasse at all (few climbers do). If you do fall in, the results may vary from trivial to fatal. Some knowledge of how to get out, and how to help a fellow climber emerge, greatly enhances the likelihood of survival.

Self-Rescue, Aided by Team

Self-rescue presupposes that you are uninjured or only slightly hurt. It does not imply that your teammates contribute no help. At the very least, a belay gives moral and physical support. It may supply the assistance without which self-rescue would be impossible. After falling, assess your position and inform those above. Make sure they have a chance to set up a good belay before you move. If you are on snow or can be lowered to a ledge, move with care lest you fall further. If you are not wearing all the warm clothing you have with you, try to put it on right away. Outward-sloping walls may provide an easy exit, or ice cliffs might be close enough together for chimneying. You may have to prussik up the rope as in Figure 24 (described in Chapter 2). If you are dangling in space, get the weight off the waist loop as soon as you can. Place one of the prearranged prussik slings in such a position that you can put one foot into it. Stand in this loop, arrange the remaining prussiks, and ascend quickly before the cold and strain sap your strength.

Team members above should set up belays and anchors to protect themselves and each other from falling into the same or other crevasses. They should analyze the terrain, work from the lower lip on steep slopes, and avoid knocking snow or gear onto the victim. The rope will tend to cut into an overhanging lip of snow; this cutting can be minimized by placing rolled-up clothing or a well-anchored ice axe between the rope and the snow.

A rescue method which is similar, but faster and less strenuous, is the Bilgiri. Its use depends on having an extra rope or an end long enough to serve as an extra rope, with enough people to handle two ropes from above. The second rope is lowered with a loop tied in the end for a footstep. If possible pass this loop

PRUSSIK
OUT OF CREVASSE

Figure 24.

down through your waist loop. Stand in it. Adjust a prussik on your own climbing rope for your other foot, and another prussik for your chest. While your weight is on one of the ropes, those above pull up the alternate rope a short distance. Transfer your weight to the upper loop. Repeat.

Team Rescue

Injury sustained in a crevasse fall is very serious. The victim may be virtually inaccessible, and is in a bitterly cold place. This is the prime circumstance where a life may depend on an adequately large party, with at least one member who understands pulley setups for climbing rescues. Without such resources and methods, the injured person can seldom be pulled out. An inexperienced rope of two or three has little choice but to assess the situation, try to prevent additional injury, and go or send at once for outside help.

If a climbing companion disappears into a crevasse, don't panic; you can't help by joining him. If there are two or more climbers above, divide the belaying, investigating, anchoring, etc. If you are alone, especially if the fallen climber can't communicate with you, there is real trouble. You have to free yourself from the rope or eventually fall in too. Try to secure the victim with an anchor. One method is to drive an axe deep into the snow through the small loop previously placed in the rope. Another method is to attach a sling to the climbing rope with a prussik, and drop it over the axe. Back up your anchors with flukes or pitons. Anchor the victim whether or not he is supported by a ledge. If he is on the rope and you cannot anchor him without slipping, let him down slowly in the hope that he will land on a ledge or snowbank.

When you are free to do so, inspect the accident site. If safe, enter the crevasse by climbing, rappelling, or prussiking down to one side of the victim (to avoid knocking down snow). Take what equipment you have, including an axe if available. Examine the injured person, give first aid, dress and pad him in all available clothing. If he is not well secured above, anchor him to his axe, an ice piton, or a bollard chopped in the ice. His crampons should be removed to help keep his feet warm. All these procedures should be followed also if some have gone for help and others remain at the site.

Going for Outside Help

If an injured or uninjured person is in a crevasse and cannot be extricated, someone must go for help. For a two-man rope the remaining one must go alone and should have an axe. Mark the accident site as clearly as you can for either ground or air search by laying expendable equipment and clothing out in a conspicuous pattern. If there are two who are free to move, and the terrain is feasible for solo climbing, one person should stay with a victim who is still alive. Fix the general location in mind by landmarks, and compass readings if possible, to avoid needless delays in rescue. You may have to go clear to a ranger station or sheriff's office, where officials will summon a rescue team or otherwise provide assistance. It is important that you speed the rescue by giving directions for finding the site of the accident, and that you give complete information as to what will probably be found.

Crevasses are the most characteristic hazard of glacier climbing. Several other problems which are encountered elsewhere are intensified on glaciers. The most important of these are coping with bad weather and keeping track of the route for a safe return. They are interrelated.

WEATHER PROBLEMS ON GLACIERS

Weather is frequently unstable in the mountains, and especially so in glacier regions. Large snow and ice masses attract and create storms. Glaciers provide very little chance of shelter. Visibility can become extremely poor on large snow surfaces devoid of landmarks. To lessen the chance of being caught in a storm, familiarize yourself with the probable weather in particular areas. Heed forecasts, and don't let wishful thinking obliterate good sense. Turn back when good or borderline weather turns bad. Wear adequate clothing and have extra garments that are warm and dry in the pack, including socks. If a storm hits, put your extra clothes on *before* you get chilled.

In a snowstorm or just a thick fog on glaciers, visibility can quickly drop to nil. A snow expanse in a dense fog exudes a sort of dancing emptiness in which it may be difficult even to tell up from down, let alone see your way. It is a wise climber who has made provisions to find his way back.

MARKING RETURN ROUTES

On glaciers it is often important to return exactly the way you came. This is because of dangers, difficulties, or length of alternate routes; because of crevasses; or because a key spot for leaving the glacier is more easily spotted from below than above. Large white expanses minus landmarks are confusing at best, and can seem hopeless in storm, fog, or darkness. Hence precautionary measures should be taken to help retrace your footsteps.

This may not be possible. Footsteps and axe holes may remain plain for days; they may never show at all if the surface is icy or pocked with irregularities that uncannily resemble footprints; or they may start out deep and unmistakable, yet disappear shortly in sun or wind.

As in all climbing, every member of the party should habitually observe landmarks, both close and far away, and behind as well as ahead. A compass is valuable if you take an occasional bearing on a landmark. At the very least you will know the general direction to be taken on the return. (Climbers have become so confused that they came down the opposite sides of peaks.) Knowing the direction in which you want to go, in poor visibility follow an approximate compass bearing by lining up the climber or climbers ahead.

A more specific way to mark a route is with wands made in advance from three- or four-foot bamboo garden stakes topped with small red or orange fluorescent banners. The sight of an occasional wand on a featureless route is reassuring. In especially obscure or vital portions of the route, the wands should be stuck into the snow a rope length apart, so when one is located the party can be sure of finding the next. Major turns or crevasses can be identified by sticking two wands in the snow. And so, it is hoped, a successful return is made from a successful climb.

Snow, ice, and glacier climbs with experienced companions enable you to build up increasing knowledge, through participation and observation, until you can assume responsibility for yourself and others. Long before this stage—and long after—you will be enjoying complete mountain ascents.

6

Preparing for Mountain Ascents: Planning, Approach, and High Camp

THERE are very few climbing areas in North America where climbers can step from their cars and in a couple of hours be in position to rope up for major ascents. Most mountaineering involves a backpack, often a long hard one, to establish a camp high enough so you can reach a summit and return to your sleeping bag in one day. Hence considerable planning and preparation are usually needed just to get within reach of technical routes on big peaks.

PLANNING A CLIMB

Whether with a club or a private group, an inexperienced climber may not realize how much planning is done by experienced friends to help ensure safety, success, and enjoyment on a climb. Many things require forethought and preparation.

Selection of Peak and Route

The decision of what to climb is based on a number of things, including challenge, accessibility, the time at your disposal, whim, and suitability and appeal for the particular climbers. Information about the objective can be gleaned from other climbers, climbers' guidebooks, and Forest Service and topographical maps.

Except for miles of backpacking, climbers seldom refer to distances as such. Pertinent statistics are given in elevations, elevation gains, and approximate number of hours along the way.

Selection of Climbing Party

Club climbs are usually scheduled months ahead of time, and supervised by leaders who are familiar with the area and who have the know-how and authority to limit participation to those qualified. Such restrictions are based largely on safety. Requirements differ from club to club and from climb to climb, and are fairly flexible; if you are new in a group, inquire. Leaders of club climbs are ordinarily chosen for their ability to make decisions and cope with problems. Under such informal but helpful supervision, an interested novice can gain experience quickly and safely.

Private climbing parties should apply similar principles in their own choice of personnel. They have more leeway, in that they can tailor the party to suit the climb, or the climb to suit the experience and physical fitness of the party. The traditional number to provide a margin of safety is a minimum of three people. If considerable roped rock climbing will be involved, two two-man ropes are usually ideal. Too large a group may be awkward to keep track of, and dangerous if all are on the same route. A party of two, or a solo climber, must recognize and compensate for the risks of having no backup group; they should stay within their established climbing abilities, and exercise prudence. The disadvantages of a small number are at times offset by the pleasures of privacy and solitude, or the speed and efficiency of a well-matched pair.

Choice of Clothing and Climbing Equipment

When information has been assembled about approach and climb, clothing and climbing equipment can be selected. Clothing for mountain ascents, even on rock routes, will be similar to that listed under snow and ice climbing in Chapter 4 because of temperatures and weather conditions at high elevations (about 8000 or 9000 feet up to 14,500 feet in the continental United States). Mountaineering boots are usually essential; and, except for very difficult rock routes, are customarily worn on remote climbs in preference to packing in rock shoes. A group should confer as to needed climbing equipment to be sure to have what is needed without much overlap. Keep in mind that at higher elevations or in poor weather, routes seem more difficult than near sea level or on a warm day. It won't do to run short of essentials, but climbing gear is far too heavy to take along in unlimited amounts.

Much of the planning and preparation involves the same problems whether the outing is for two days or two weeks. But the farther you go from civilization and the longer you plan to stay, the more you need to be self-sufficient—and this includes the knowledge and equipment to avoid or cope with trouble.

MISHAPS AND EMERGENCIES

Accidents in the mountains are rare among experienced mountaineers who have come to understand and adjust to their environment and their own abilities. Dangers which are environmental are considered "objective": storms, lightning, crevasses, falling rocks, and other natural conditions over which the climber has no direct control. Hazards inherent primarily in the climber rather than in the environment are called "subjective": poor judgment, overconfidence, slips, inadequate preparation, lack of proper physical conditioning, illness, and the like. Learning to understand, forecast, avoid, or deal with potential dangers greatly increases the safety and satisfaction of mountaineering.

Several specific things not already mentioned can be done at home to increase your competence on trips:

(1) Keep in good physical condition.

(2) Study first aid, with particular attention to lacerations, bleed-

ing, head and spinal injuries, dislocations, broken bones, frost-bite, and shock.

(3) Learn at least rudimentary techniques for rescues. Many climbing clubs and search and rescue organizations arrange demonstrations and practice.

Safety Precautions on Trips

The following additional points are valuable to help you keep out of trouble or do something constructive about it:

(1) Before each trip, leave word of your plans with someone who will really notice and act if you don't return. Write down your itinerary and expected time of return. Add the name of a climbing friend, ranger station, or sheriff to notify if necessary. Those at home should not panic if the party is a few hours or even a day overdue, as minor delays are often unavoidable.

(2) Have extra supplies in the car: water, food, spare clothing and shoes, and perhaps a blanket.

(3) Carry first aid supplies. Have a kit of your own, and be sure one is carried on your rope. It should be stocked with an antiseptic; aspirin or equivalent; codeine or some other painkiller prescribed by a physician; adhesive tape and sterile gauze bandages and pads; a single-edged razor blade or a small pair of scissors that really cut; elastic bandage for sprains; and a splint (at least above timberline)—compact types can be inflatable or of hardware cloth. Waterproof matches, pencil, paper, and safety pins might be added.

(4) Make it a habit to pay attention to your surroundings.

(5) Use common sense as to weather, giving up a climb, etc.

(6) Suspect altitude sickness, caused by shortage of oxygen, if someone becomes listless or nauseated at elevations from about 10,000 feet up. It is often so mild that it can be cured by time, rest, deep breathing, or a little easily digested food. Recovery may be spontaneous or quick, occur overnight, or not take place until descent to a lower elevation.

(7) Regard as serious a sudden dry cough and breathing difficulty. These may be early signs of pulmonary edema, rare at moderate altitudes but extremely urgent. The victim must be helped to a lower elevation at once.

(8) Prevent hypothermia. This condition, formerly termed "exposure," is a dangerous lowering of the body temperature, usually from a combination of wet, cold, fatigue, and lack of food. The wind-chill factor is especially important; even a light wind has the effect of lowering temperatures radically, especially when clothing is wet.

Hypothermia has been called "the killer of the unprepared"; this is accurate, but not exclusively so. People amply supplied with spare gear have died because they did not recognize the insidious onset of the condition. They delayed putting on dry warm clothing until they were so confused and chilled that it was impossible. Take spare clothes, and don them as soon as you start to feel cold. Take extra food and eat frequently. Keep dry if you can. Camp quickly if you must. Exercise is normally warming, but not past the point of exhaustion.

Individuals differ. Help a companion who is shivering uncontrollably or seems befuddled, even if he tries to reject aid. You must warm him up with dry clothes next to his body, shelter, fire, hot drinks and other food, a sleeping bag, or your own body heat. Don't leave him alone—his judgment is temporarily gone. If his temperature drops too low, he will die.

(9) In minor accidents, make every effort to help yourself, or to assist a member of your party, rather than summoning outside help. Outside rescue is time-consuming, expensive, and if unneeded is an imposition on others.

Trouble the Party Cannot Cope With

If self-rescue is impossible or may compound an injury, or if a major accident occurs, you must get outside help. Keep your head. The first thing to do is to figure out how to help the injured person immediately. Get him to a safe place and try to determine the extent of his injuries. Give him first aid if indicated. An open wound should be kept clean. Try to keep the victim warm.

Someone must go for help, either a member of the climbing party or another person in the vicinity. If at all possible, somebody should stay with the injured person. If this is not possible, he should be tied on securely if in a spot where he could fall or wander away. The person summoning assistance should travel quickly, but with care. The best place to find help is a ranger station or sheriff's office. Give complete information as to the location of the accident, the condition of the victim, and what aid is required. (It is best to have this written down so none of it is forgotten.) In many climbing areas, the authorities will summon nearby volunteer or official rescue groups who have the manpower, equipment, and training to deal with such emergencies.

While waiting for help, bend all efforts toward keeping the victim alive and as comfortable as possible. If the party is large enough, get him a sleeping bag from camp. Provide water and food. Try to keep up his morale. It may be a long wait.

BACKPACKING AND CAMPING EQUIPMENT FOR CLIMBERS

Camping equipment for long rugged trips must be light and sturdy, and be kept to a minimum. A general aim on difficult backpacks is to take everything you need and nothing you don't. Necessary items are discussed here.

Packframe

A well-designed packframe makes it possible to carry heavy loads with a reasonable degree of comfort (though sixty pounds is still sixty pounds). The best packframes are of tubular aluminum, with nylon fittings. A waist strap or wrap-around feature permits the load to be supported largely on the hips. Climbers of your acquaintance can recommend a good brand of packframe. It will be expensive but very durable. Choose the right size for your height and build. It should have a generous sack, and roomy outer pockets for trail needs.

Many climbers prefer extra lightweight "internal" packframes which have thin aluminum or even graphite struts integrated into the padding. The struts can be bent to conform to the exact contours of *your* back. The fit is tighter and allows more maneuverability—a real plus on difficult or brushy terrain.

Sleeping Bag

Nights in climbing camps are often cold. A down bag is generally accepted as the only kind that is sufficiently warm, light, and compact; but anything filled with down must be kept fairly dry. Bags partly or wholly filled with a spun synthetic fiber that absorbs little water are used in wet areas; good results have been reported. A medium-priced bag with two or three pounds of prime goose down should keep you warm. A mummy case design that covers the head, and tapers at head and foot, makes the most efficient use of the down. More roomy bags, also long enough to cover the head, can be gathered about the face with a drawstring. The lightest strong casing material is rip-stop nylon. The zipper should be heavy duty, insulated with a baffle. The bag should be of box or tube construction, not sewn through. Sleeping bags are usually crammed into stuff bags for backpacking, and should be well shaken up before use on cold nights. Between trips, store well fluffed up to maintain the loft.

Mattress and Groundsheet

Carry a plastic or waterproofed nylon groundsheet. Take a mattress approximately two by four feet in size. Clothing and equipment go under the head and feet. A pad of closed-cell foam such as urethane, about one-and-one-half inches thick, is comfortable and light but somewhat bulky. Urethane absorbs moisture and should have a protective cover. Closed-cell pads (ensolite), about three-eighths inch thick, are waterproof, compact, and good insulation (as when sleeping on snow), but are not soft. Air mattresses are compact, and comfortable if not overinflated, but are prone to leak.

Shelter

Climbers usually take some sort of shelter, no matter how sketchy. A one-man plastic tube about nine feet long and three feet in diameter can be pitched anywhere you can rig a ridgeline. Equipment or rounded stones placed inside hold down the edges. The tube's main disadvantage is condensation inside. Never close the ends—suffocation may result. Another type of lightweight shelter, suitable for two or more, can be rigged from a nine-by-twelve-foot sheet of plastic (such as a painter's drop cloth) or a coated nylon tarp. Take cord for pitching, and a groundsheet.

A lightweight tent with a rain fly and sewn-in floor is desirable or necessary in areas and seasons of heavy precipitation or cold wind. A tent also keeps out insects and affords privacy. A good backpacking tent is a considerable monetary investment and should be chosen with care. Consult others. (Some designs that sound good on paper are real duds in camp.) Consider size, shape, weight, height, poles, etc., and try pitching it before buying. Many outing stores provide tent-pitching facilities on the premises.

PERSONAL AND MISCELLANEOUS EQUIPMENT

Various miscellaneous items should be carried by every climber. These include dark glasses or goggles, pocketknife, watch, matches in waterproof container, fire starter (three or four heat tabs, canned heat, or candle stub), flashlight, handkerchief, and adhesive bandages. Also take sunburn preventive, lip salve, and insect repellent if season and location make them necessary.

Equip your flashlight with alkaline batteries. Reverse one battery when light is in the pack, to prevent drain of current if the switch is accidentally pushed to "on." Also keep materials handy for taping up sore spots on your feet as soon as you notice them (adhesive tape or moleskin, and lamb's wool to pad blisters). Have toilet paper (plenty) in pockets and pack. In the pack, include needle and thread, or at least safety pins, and toilet articles (toothbrush, comb, maybe a small mirror, towel, and soap). Include personal prescription drugs. Women should take any personal supplies they may need.

Group or Individual Miscellany

These articles (some optional) may be individual or community equipment: camera and film, route information, maps and compass, plastic or aluminum water bottle, folding pocket cup (sometimes water cannot be reached without one), pencil and paper, and first aid kit.

COOKING EQUIPMENT

Climbers sometimes like to cook individually, but more often plan group meals. The following list covers equipment that is really needed for high-camp cookery, including a few items that may be omitted:

Pots, two; a one-quart or a quart-and-a-half size are about right for two or three people. A pot gripper is preferred by many to rigid or bail handles. Wooden or plastic handles may burn up if cooking is done over a fire.

Covers, one or two. They hasten cooking, keep debris out of food, and can double as frying pans or plates.

Cups, one apiece; metal, enamel, or plastic.

Spoons, one apiece; dessert or tablespoon size.

Rags or paper towels, to use as pot holders, dishtowels, etc.

Matches, some in waterproof container in pocket, many in pack.

Can opener, midget GI or roll type (if you take cans).

Container for carrying water a long distance; collapsible plastic water bottle or large canteen. Unneeded where a campsite near water can be counted on.

Stove, one-burner pressure or cartridge type.

Extra fuel for stove (liquid fuel should be carried in a metal can with pouring spout, filters, and tight cap). Carry the fuel can in an outside pocket of your pack to lessen the chance of fumes reaching your food.

Stoves and Fires

In many alpine and subalpine areas, especially where firewood is scarce and campsites much overused, open fires are no longer permitted. This and related regulations are discussed in Chapter 8. Cooking on a small one-burner pressure stove will help to protect the fragile mountain environment from destruction. A stove, moreover, is very convenient. You can camp above or below timberline, avoid sooty pots, cook in the tent in inclement weather, and be reasonably sure of a hot breakfast (in bed?) *and* a quick start on climbing mornings.

There are numerous good lightweight backpacking stoves on the market. See which ones your friends prefer under local conditions. Some stoves burn white gasoline (unleaded, but *not* the same as "leadfree"). Kerosene is less volatile than gasoline, hence harder to start. Butane and propane stoves fueled by cartridges are convenient, but the cartridges are not as universally available as petroleum products. Follow the directions that come with the stove! Understand all possible foibles of the appliance before you leave home. If a stove has been unused for some time, try it out before a trip. Extra fuel must usually be carried. Keep gasoline and kerosene at a discreet distance from food, both in the pack and out of it. If you carry in cartridges, be sure to carry out the empties. One small stove is adequate for three or four people.

If you plan on open fires in an area where they are permitted and wood is prolific, find out whether a fire permit is required. Climbers rarely carry a woodsman's axe; they burn dead wood. Build the fire on sand or rock (*not* on humus) and well away from logs and trees. Use an existing fireplace if there is one, or construct a small simple one of rocks placed so your pot can span them. Keep the fire small. And before you leave camp, be sure the fire is *drowned out,* and cold to the touch.

FOOD

Food is a bulky and weighty necessity. The total mass decreases with each day of a trip, but the groceries must be chosen with care for several reasons. Climbing leaves scant time and energy for cooking, and even scant interest in it if appetites grow picky with altitude and exhaustion. High camp conditions frequently fall short of ideal for meal preparation—what with crotchety stoves, skimpy fuel supplies, icy water, cold wind, frequent mealtime darkness, and low boiling points (water boils at 198 degrees at 7500 feet, 194 degrees at 10,000 feet, and so on). Although an occasional enthusiast declares that climbing and gourmet cooking can and should co-exist, they usually do not.

Types and Amounts of Food to Take

Select food you like, but make sure it is quick and simple to prepare and eat. It should be largely dehydrated, concentrated in bulk and food value, durable, and proof against spoilage. Although cooking time roughly doubles with every 5000 feet of elevation gain, anything supposed to cook at a simmer in a few minutes ought to be satisfactory. Include foods that can be eaten uncooked or just warmed up.

Individual needs vary as to daily amount of food. Teenagers and other bottomless eaters can consume two or more pounds of concentrated, dehydrated food per day, and still be ravenously hungry. Light eaters can perhaps get by on one pound per day. Average eaters may find a pound and a half enough. There is always the specter of having to carry it in.

Some fat in the menu is desirable, but at times seems hard to digest under climbing conditions. Proteins (meat, cheese, etc.) digest more readily than fats, and stick to the ribs longer than carbohydrates. Carbohydrates (starches and sugars) provide quick energy and are easiest to digest. Carbohydrate-rich meals seem to increase both mental and physical efficiency at elevations of around 10,000, according to military and other tests, and also according to most climbers' individual reactions.

An active person needs 3000 to 5000 calories a day; but this hardly seems worth analyzing for a few days' trip. Forget calories, judge amounts by total weights and past experience, take a few vitamin pills if you so desire, and eat heartily when you get back home.

Menu Planning and Groceries

For short trips of two or three days, take anything you want to, as long as it won't cause food poisoning by the time you eat it. For longer trips, detailed planning of meals is necessary, to be reasonably sure the food will come out even. Make a list of prospective campsites and the elevations. Consider the method of cooking, activities planned, personal tastes, and appetites. Make out a menu for every meal (not necessarily followed later). From the menu list, make your grocery list. Include plenty of salt, as you may lose a lot through bodily dehydration. Allow some food for emergencies. Keep your lists (with notations added after trips) for future reference. Good meals for climbing trips can be assembled by following these suggestions:

Breakfasts. Start active days with small breakfasts. Large ones are time-consuming to prepare, and most climbers find a full stomach a liability, especially about 4 a.m. A satisfactory climbing breakfast can be made up of cold or "stir and serve" hot cereal, with sugar and dried milk; and a hot beverage such as cocoa, instant coffee, or tea. Gourmets could consider a few hearty, time-consuming breakfasts for days in camp—freeze-dried scrambled eggs, bacon, pancakes with brown sugar syrup, etc.

Lunches. Instead of one large lunch, eat a series of snacks on trail and climb. Keep some lunch food in your pocket, so you can eat a bite whenever you want to. Lunch foods can be bread or tough crackers, natural cheeses (processed cheese spoils), hard sausage, jerky, nuts, raisins, fig bars, candy (some hard; lemon drops taste good), and lemonade or iced tea mixes. Some climbers put all ingredients (except the beverage) in a sack together; the result is "gorp."

Dinners. Quickest and easiest to cook and eat are one-pot concoctions. For a good mixture, stir a quick-cooking dried soup mix into water, and at appropriate intervals add some of these nutritional and thickening agents: macaroni, cheese, sausage chunks, potato powder, canned meat or fish, instant rice, chipped beef, noodles, margarine (keeps better than butter, and provides calories, flavor, and the day's fat), and seasonings. Many of these ingredients can be served separately for variety, or eaten as-is when cooking becomes impossible. If time and energy are unusually short, try some of the pre-cooked freeze-dried "main dishes" that are ready as soon as hot water is poured into the container. Dehydrated or freeze-dried fruits make good desserts, and so do cookies. More complicated dinners can be fixed on rest days. Experiment with some of the freeze-dried vegetables and meats. (What a miracle to watch pieces of cardboard turn into beefsteaks and pork chops!)

Where to Buy Climbing Foods

Suitable foods can be obtained in supermarkets, in backpacking and mountaineering shops, or often by mail order from mountaineering outlets. Many dehydrated foods can be found in supermarkets, but be sure to read the directions to find out if they are suitable for your camping conditions. Mountaineering shops carry an enormous variety of freeze-dried foods that are lightweight, convenient, and often unobtainable elsewhere—but they are costly. A combination of backpacking and supermarket foods gives a good variety at a reasonable price.

Repackaging and Protecting Food

Foods sold especially for backpacking are nearly always well packaged. The containers of supermarket groceries, however, are generally so bulky, and protect the food so poorly, that repackaging is desirable. Also, small amounts taken from the kitchen staples need special treatment. In the main, use plastic sacks closed with string or rubber bands, or use sacks with sliding closures. Label the bags as to contents, and include any needed directions cut from the original package. Food which has already been put up in sturdy plastic or foil envelopes should be kept that way, and small items can be grouped inside larger plastic sacks. Cereals, instant coffee, salt, and sugar may need an inner cloth sack to prevent disaster in case of a puncture. Margarine can be carried in a screw-top aluminum can. While you are on the move, it is handy to have the food sorted by meals. For camp, it is adequate to bag things by category. Keep an eye on the diminishing supplies in case rationing is required toward the end of a trip.

In camp, food needs some extra care. Foods that need refrigeration can be put in shade (always cool at high elevations), in a stream, or in a snowbank—but all these methods are fallible, as the sun moves, snow melts, etc. If storing food in a kettle, put a good rock on the cover. Theoretically, plastic sacks are rainproof, but they tend to acquire holes, and should be put under shelter when you leave camp. Bears, deer, and rodents such as ground squirrels, pikas, and porcupines may feast on your food. Put all food in a bag and hang it well above the ground if a suitable tree or overhanging rock is available. Otherwise, bury the food bag in your pack or cover it with rocks and hope for the best.

APPROACH AND HIGH CAMP

The number of things to take, for high camp and climb, seems a little overwhelming at first, but it all consolidates. To remember everything, keep a detailed list. Check it before every trip. You cannot believe, until it happens, how easily you can forget the most obvious things—boots, matches, sleeping bag. Time is saved if packs are made up as completely as possible at home.

Backpacking Pace

Start up the trail slowly; your second wind will come. You cannot dawdle on long approaches, but to hurry is folly. You can go only as fast as lungs and legs permit, a speed that varies from person to person and depends on such factors as physical conditioning, type of trail, and elevation. The most efficient pace is one you can maintain for hours with an occasional pause to get your breath and a few longer rests to eat, drink, and enjoy the view. Excessively long rests waste time and make it hard to re-establish an economical rhythm. A determined slogging will take you farther, sooner, than spurts and collapses. Keep your mind on the surroundings instead of on sore feet.

Terrain Problems on the Approach

A trail is the easiest approach, and sometimes goes clear to the high camp. Don't leave it until you must—and don't wreck that precious trail by shortcuts, a major cause of erosion on switchbacks. At some point, the party must often take off across rough, steep, cross-country going. From here on, keep in touch with each other. Take the most open brush-free route you can find.

Cross streams with caution. Look for narrow places that can be safely jumped, stepping stones, logs that provide a teetery bridge, or broad shallow fords. Wading in boots is safer than going barefoot. For a fast or high stream, belay the first and last man, and fix the rope as a handline for others. If you are not carrying an ice axe, use a strong pole for a staff. Streams flowing from glaciers and snowfields are lower in the morning than in the afternoon. Not all streams can be crossed—turn back in preference to drowning.

Selecting and Protecting High Camp

On a typical weekend trip, the first day is usually spent packing in and the second climbing and packing out. If you have the luxury of three days, you can pack in the first, climb the second, and pack out the third.

The campsite is a fairly inflexible goal, as close as practical to the technical climbing. For a standard route, it will probably be a traditional spot. For a new or seldom-made route, study maps, consult other climbers, calculate route length and difficulty, and inspect the terrain from a distance; on arrival, find the exact campsite. Once established, your camp seems like a cozy home in a superb location.

Keep it as lovely as you find it. Protect your water. Soap, old socks, toothpaste, and human wastes don't belong in high mountain creeks and tarns—nor groundsheets among the gentians. When you leave, burn what trash you can, and *carry out* all foil and plastic (they never decompose), and any cans or stove cartridges. Leave your campsite as clean as (or cleaner than) you found it.

High Camp Living

Basic requirements for a climbing camp are few: sleeping spots; means of erecting a shelter; firewood if you have no stove and open fires are permitted; and drinking water.

Bed and Shelter. Choose sleeping sites for warmth and flatness. Air temperatures are warmest well above the level of streams and meadows, since cold air flows downhill at night. Meadow camping should be a last resort anyway, as high meadows are very fragile (and frequently wet). Dry ground is warmer than wet, though sleeping on snow can be more snug than it sounds. A bed for one can be a very small flat spot. If several are to share a shelter, a bigger place must be found or made. Improve a prospective bed site, if required, by prying out the most ill-placed rocks; use your axe if you must. Give a thought to drainage—a bed built below a sort of funnel can be a disaster that even ditching can't remedy if it rains.

For a tube, a tent minus poles, or a fly, you have to place your bed among boulders or trees to which you can hitch the ridgeline. Flies can be erected in a multitude of designs, usually shed- or A-shaped. If there are no grommets, tie the cords tightly around little bunches of the plastic at corners and sides, and fasten the other ends tautly to rocks or whatever. Pitch shelters fairly tight to cut down on their whipping in the wind or collecting pools of rainwater. Frequent readjustment is often necessary. If the plastic tears, mend it promptly with adhesive tape.

Place your stove in a cozy nook sheltered from the wind.

Drinking Water. In past years it was assumed that water from mountain lakes, tarns, streams, and snowfields was safe to drink. Its purity can no longer be taken for granted. In some areas, mountain water supplies, even drips from snow banks, have become polluted by an intestinal parasite, *Giardia lamblia*, spread by people or wild animals. The symptoms of Giardiasis are very unpleasant and often long-lasting. Seemingly not everyone who has drunk the polluted water gets sick. But those who do, experience symptoms that include explosive diarrhea and related miseries. The symptoms typically appear seven to ten days after exposure. The sooner medical treatment is obtained, the better for the victim.

Prevention is advisable if possible. Chlorine treatment of the water appears to be ineffective, and treatment with iodine seems open to some doubt. The most reliable method appears to be boiling all drinking water in an area where the parasite has been proven or suspected. This is a great nuisance, but is advisable. Boil the water actively for at least one minute at sea level, and much longer at higher elevations.

Your sleeping bags are invitingly fluffed up under the shelter. The stove's small circle of blue flame is whispering or roaring beneath the pot. You are steeped with content as you look out over the twilit expanse of valleys and peaks. All this and heaven too; you will climb tomorrow.

7

Climbing and Descending
the Peaks

ON A full mountain ascent, the techniques and judgments
you have learned meld together, and you gain in mountaineering
maturity on each climb. Every ascent differs from every other.
None turns out exactly as planned. But there are different patterns
in success, defeat, and disaster that establish the wisdom of knowing what you are about. Your immediate goal is reaching the
summit. Getting there and back safely and with finesse is competent mountaineering.

PREPARATIONS THE NIGHT BEFORE THE CLIMB

You usually start final preparations for the following day's climb
as soon as the high camp is established.

Making up the Ropes

A club or large private party usually camps where several peaks
or various routes are accessible. Avoid having more than one or

two ropes on the same route, especially on rock, where parties cannot spread out for efficient travel and for protection from loose rocks. The group leaders consult individuals as to wishes and abilities; ropes are made up so each includes a leader equal to the route and others to round out a safe party. If two ropes are to be on the same climb, the strongest and fastest goes first (a fast rope feels frustrated when stuck behind a slow rope that should let it pass).

Studying Routes

If the route is unfamiliar or somewhat indefinite, and is visible from camp or from a high point nearby, it should be studied by the entire party. Note key points along the route, step-by-step details, and possible alternatives going both up and down. These factors are often hard to assess when you are on the route.

Planning the Departure Time

For all but the shortest climbs and the most experienced parties, plan to start early. Climbs have a way of taking the entire day, and even more. Plan to arise or even to leave camp as soon as you can see. Morning preparations usually take an hour. Calculate the probable time between departure and return. Some of the elements involved are elevation gain; the altitude; what proportions of the climb are technical and non-technical; overall difficulty; how long it has taken previous parties (and who they were); and the size, speed, and condition of the present party, especially the slowest person. In general, non-technical climbing is faster than technical; experienced climbers speedier than neophytes; and a small group swifter than a big one. Allow extra time for stops and for the unexpected. Roughly half of the ascent time should be allowed for the descent.

An exceptionally early start is sometimes advisable. For instance, an established weather pattern of afternoon storms in the area may make it desirable to complete a route early. A glacier climb may begin around midnight, as sometimes a portion of the route must be covered before the sun starts icefalls and rockfalls, or afternoon snow conditions may promise to be particularly bad.

Getting back to camp early in the day is a delight. Returning in time to cook dinner before dark is beneficial though not necessary. Being caught out in complete darkness is inconceivably time-consuming, and sometimes stops you—cold!

Organizing for the Climb

The bare necessities that must be left until morning will take quite long enough; do all you can the night before. Make up your pack, putting in everything not needed overnight. (Add the rest next morning.) Include climbing equipment, food, maps, flashlight, first aid kit, water bottle, extra clothing, dry socks in a plastic bag, matches and fire starter, and camera (if desired). Remove useless items from your pockets, and put things in that you will need in the early morning and on the climb: sunburn dope, lip balm, dark glasses, knife, handkerchief, compass, mittens, watch, toilet paper, adhesive bandages, and folding cup.

If you plan to leave a note in camp regarding your route, write it now. Sort out the breakfast things, and put the rest of the food away. Sleeping in part of your clothing makes getting up a little less obnoxious. Go to bed early. After a long backpack, insomnia is unlikely, and bed is the best place to keep warm.

EARLY MORNING PREPARATIONS

There is always one dependable (but unpopular) climber who wakes up by the appointed hour and rouses the others. Before getting up, inspect the weather. Storm, or clearly impending storm, rules out climbing. Good or indecisive weather compels you to arise. A climb is often approached in uncertain weather that later becomes beautiful. The atmosphere around camp is usually silent and gloomy before dawn as climbers groggily perform their chores; the thought of climbing may seem distasteful or even ominous at this hour.

When to Stay in Camp

Weather influences the plans of the whole party. Indisposition is a personal matter, though it may indirectly affect your friends.

If you are really ill, do not go; even using willpower, you could not fail to be a liability on the climb. If you just "don't feel very good," say so but start out; very often you recover after an hour or so. If not, you can turn back alone while still on easy ground close to camp.

Leaving Camp in Order

To make reasonably sure of finding all in good order when you return to camp, leave it so. Put all food away. Leave sleeping bags loosely rolled, under the shelter and on top of the mattresses. If you have only a groundsheet, roll everything up in that and weight the wad down with rocks. Showers and winds come and go often. Place rocks on odds and ends such as spoons, soap, and anything that might blow away or be carried off by industrious varmints.

Identifying Campsite

Your camp may be so distinctively situated that you can spot it even from the summit. Or it may merge into the landscape. Each climber should fix its location firmly in his mind in relation to major landmarks, tree line, stream courses, etc. Further, when leaving camp you might construct one or more unmistakable cairns at conspicuous spots to indicate that camp is near. Look back from time to time and implant its location in your mind.

TERRAIN BETWEEN CAMP AND ROPING-UP POINT

From high camp there is usually an extension of the approach before roped climbing begins. This may be over meadows, moraines, easy slabs, snow-filled basins and chutes, and increasingly steep slopes of tumbled talus blocks.

Talus

Talus slopes consist of rock fragments which have piled up below cliffs, usually in gullies that fan out at the bottom. The

Figure 25. Approaching the climb. (Courtesy of Swiss National Tourist Office, New York.)

blocks often start at about house or car size, and as you climb diminish to fist or pea size. The larger pieces are usually well consolidated—but watch out for the occasional rocker. The smaller ones on steep slopes may be very loose. Nimble leaping and long steps are required for the first; use your axe for balance or feel, but keep the loop off your wrist. On the loose parts, go up the firmest portions you can find. The axe is helpful as a staff. Adjacent snow slopes are often far preferable to the talus, unless they are too icy for the equipment you have available. A route along the foot of the cliff, where you can use occasional handholds, is sometimes easier than the center of the gully. On loose talus where occasional rocks are kicked down in spite of reasonable care, the group should spread out horizontally so no one is directly below others. If this is impossible, all should keep close together so rolling rocks cannot gain enough momentum to be hazardous.

Pace

As when backpacking, the climber should not push himself to go faster than his breathing and leg muscles permit. Leg movements and breathing do not always coincide on steep going. Momentum is often necessary for a smooth move, followed by a pause to catch your breath. A slow start does not mean you will be slow all day, but increasing elevation naturally imposes limitations on speed. Each climber should proceed at his own optimum rate on non-technical ground, but the faster ones should keep in touch with the slower ones.

Rests

Usually the first hour requires a pause to tighten boot laces, remove surplus garments, etc. When the sun comes up, make another stop to put on sunburn goop and dark glasses. Within a couple of hours, the first lunch is needed. Tank up on water at every opportunity unless you suspect it is contaminated (see *Selecting and Protecting High Camp* in Chapter 6); it is likely to be scarce or absent later. Fill the water bottle before you run out of streams. Use each stop to scan whatever you can see of the route. Make all stops brief. The extra hours may be badly needed at the end of the day.

ROPING UP

The real climb begins when you rope. From now on, you are not climbing as individuals but as a team.

When to Rope

Obviously the rope is needed when steep and exposed cliffs begin, or when the party steps out on a glacier. Less obviously, you should rope for borderline rocks which may be fairly easy, but are so loose or so exposed that a slip could not be stopped. If you want to tie on before the others do, say so; it is false pride to climb unroped if you feel insecure, and can result in injury or death.

Reorganizing Equipment

At the roping-up point, arrange all equipment for technical climbing. On climbs where all ice and snow end at the point where rock begins, you may be able to safely leave crampons and axes. Cache them in a spot protected from falling rocks, such as under an overhang; be sure they won't fall off, and be very sure you can find them on your return. Take them along, however, if there is any chance of their being needed above (snow and ice on ledges are often invisible from below), or of your returning by a different route.

Carrying Ice Axe and Crampons on Rock

If axe and crampons will not be needed for some time, they should be stowed away on or in the pack. Most packs have loops and/or straps for carrying the axe, spike uppermost. If you will use the axe intermittently, clip it to your waist loop or a sling by the carabiner hole (if any), let it dangle from your wrist by its loop, carry it in a belt holster, stick it down between your back and pack (if any), or stick it through your waist loop—remembering that it is a lethal hazard if you fall. If it gets in the way when belaying on rock, lay it in a very safe place nearby.

In mixed going where rock and snow alternate frequently, crampons may be worn for short stretches on rock, but should be removed for long stretches both to protect the points and for climbing efficiency. The crampons can be carried in or tied to the outside of the pack, but the points should be sheathed in either case.

THE TECHNICAL CLIMB

The climbing itself, whether on rock, snow, or both, is essentially what you have been doing in practice areas. Psychologically it differs because it is part of a much larger enterprise. The remoteness of your location heightens the sense of challenge, adventure, independence, and accomplishment. It also demands sharpened techniques, caution, and attention to natural surroundings. Several features of high-mountain conditions differ, at least in emphasis, from those in more accessible climbing areas.

Continuous Climbing

Easy and difficult climbing often alternate on intricate routes. After the rope is put on, it is usually removed only for very long easy stretches. On portions of the route that do not require a belay, except perhaps for reasons of exposure, the climbers remain roped but all move at the same time. The leader holds one or two coils in his hand. The second and third are responsible for the rope in front of them. They coil enough to leave ten or fifteen feet between climbers. Each must be considerate in adapting his pace to that of the others on terrain of uneven difficulty. The climbing may be such that a slip could occur but could be easily held by the others immediately bracing themselves to take the minor shock. If one climber wants an upper belay, he should request the man ahead to stop, set a belay, and take up rope.

Route Finding

Routes in practice areas often are rigidly defined and become very familiar. On far peaks, where routes are not well known and have endless variations, the rope leader must find the way to the summit and also choose among alternative pitches. Sometimes considerable scouting is required to locate a key pitch. If possible, the leader should stay well within the climbing capacities of everyone on the rope.

Loose Rocks

In popular rock climbing areas, the rock is generally good to begin with, and over the years most loose chunks have been removed by assiduous "gardening." The high mountains always have some loose rock, usually a lot, and sometimes so much that you wonder how they stand at all.

You must learn to climb on or over it without sending fusillades down on anyone who might be below, or losing your own balance. Step fastidiously on ledges. Keep the rope from dislodging loose pieces. Move chunks lying in especially precarious positions, and put them in more secure spots. Choose your belay stances to avoid being in the line of fire from the climbing route. Test all holds, first gingerly and then more firmly. In climbing past an especially unstable rock, avoid even touching it. Learn which loose holds can stand certain pressures without being dislodged, and which are adequate for balance in conjunction with firmer holds.

Climbing Miseries

Rock climbing in particular is usually pursued most ardently under pleasant conditions. When climbing on high peaks, you must be prepared to suffer cheerfully through an array of discomforts. You are nearly always either too hot or too cold. Temperatures vary radically with the wind and from sun to shade. Rock climbing in gloves is almost impossible, so expect to climb part of the time with cold hands; wear mittens or gloves for belaying. Between the dry mountain air and lack of water, thirst may be acute. Drink any water you come to, eat available snow and icicles sparingly, and stuff snow into your water bottle before it is empty. Otherwise, forget your thirst—until the exquisite moment after the climb when you come to that first welcome stream.

Huffing and puffing and a touch of malaise are normal; ignore them. The glorious surroundings, and the concentration required by the climbing, help to keep your mind off your troubles. The hours fly by. Eventually you reach the top.

THE SUMMIT

Summits have great individuality. They range from mild-looking snow humps to soaring pinnacles. The true summit of a peak is nearly always marked with a cairn (if not, perhaps you have realized the climber's dream: a first ascent). Usually there is a register in which to record your arrival. It may be anything from a rusty tobacco tin to an imposing cast-aluminum box placed by an outdoor club. The ideal summit includes warm sunshine, a far view in every direction, and plenty of time to relax, eat, study the map, and read the register with its comments both historic and funny. True, not all are ideal; and in any event, watch the time and the weather. You are on top of the mountain, but the climb is just half over; you must return to camp.

TURNING BACK BEFORE REACHING SUMMIT

Though all your plans and efforts have been focused on reaching the top of the mountain, you occasionally must turn back sooner. Such decisions are the responsibility of the leader; but mountain climbing (except with guides) is pretty democratic. The leader should consult his companions, who usually feel free and eager to express opinions whether consulted or not. A rope *must* stay together, even if there is disagreement. On a technical climb no one should ever be left alone or desert the party, although two ropes of recognized competence can make independent decisions. There are several logical reasons for not completing an ascent.

Time

When partway up, you may compare the time taken so far with the estimated time of descent; it may be plain that you have to turn back if you are to get off the difficult portion by dark. Too late a start, a slow party, photography, lingering for fun, and miscalculation are among reasons for running out of time.

Weather

Do your best to predict the weather before going into an area, especially in ranges noted for bad weather. Consider the weatherman's five-day forecasts (for what they are worth; in some areas even three-day predictions are suspect). Find out about weather patterns in unfamiliar areas by asking for local opinions. Mountains attract and make their own weather, so study the sky during a climb. Bad weather is reason enough to give up the climb; rain, wind, and snow make both climbing conditions and climbers miserable; a climb can turn into a calamity. Lightning is a strong incentive for getting below peaks and ridges with all speed consistent with safety.

Illness and Injury

Illness on an ascent is unlikely but not impossible; it necessitates descent while the victim can still travel. A minor accident might have both a physical and a psychological effect, and may be another reason for retreat; but if there is plenty of time and the weather is good, the party can rest and think it over before deciding to go up or back down.

THE DESCENT

Going down is easier and faster than going up because you are not working against gravity. But there are problems as well as advantages. The party usually retraces its route of ascent except when there is a familiar route known to be easier. If the first man down is not sure of the route, he should consult someone who is. Unfamiliar descent routes that appear temptingly easy in the upper portions often lead to critical difficulties below; a long climb up again may result.

Caution on Descent

More accidents occur on the descent of long climbs than on the ascent. The reasons include the following: (1) The climbers' momentum is downward, so slips are more likely to occur than during the ascent. (2) The party often has a false feeling of over-confidence, elation, and relaxation after a successful climb. (3) The climbers are tired; both judgment and physical abilities may be impaired. (4) The party is in a hurry to get back to camp. (5) Conditions may be worse—the weather threatening, air cold, and the light poor. Extra care should be practiced.

Techniques of Descent

If the climbing is at all steep, the leader comes down last to protect his party. In the high mountains the party is more apt to climb down than to rappel. Routes are often poorly adapted to rappelling, and rope handling is time-consuming when climbing and rappelling frequently alternate. However, on steep difficult pitches that are particularly uninviting to climb down, a rappel may be preferred. Take special care in selecting the rappel point. Be sure the rope does not send down loose rocks; the first man down should remove any rocks that might easily be dislodged. More frequent belays may be advisable on the descent than on the ascent, and the rope is often kept on longer.

Descending Scree and Talus

On the way up, fine gravel and coarse dirt (scree) were probably avoided because of their instability. On the way down, scree should be sought out, as it forms chutes that you can slide, run, or shuffle down. The talus is just about as tedious on the descent as on the ascent, and maybe more so. Certainly, muscles used on a long descent cry out in protest next day. The large talus blocks often seem easier than in the morning, in contrast with the technical climbing.

Travel After Dark

On long climbs (perhaps because you disregarded your calculations in order to make the peak), you may be benighted. On technical terrain, climbing after dark is so dangerous that you should normally stop till morning. On non-technical ground, you can campward "plod your weary way." Go as fast as you can while you can still see, as progress is very slow after dark. Vision adjusts well in gradually failing light, and there is often enough illumination with moon, stars, snow, and pale rocks to continue without using the flashlight. On cloudy nights, in the woods, or on rather tricky footing, the time comes when you have to use the flashlight for safety. Once it is turned on, your vision no longer adjusts to the dim light beyond its beam. Travel by flashlight on uneven ground brings up a new set of inconveniences to slow down the long trek, especially because there is usually only one light per party. At least during night travel a climber makes the character-building discovery that, although his knees are literally buckling with exhaustion, he can keep right on going for as many hours as need be.

BIVOUACS

As used by climbers, to "bivouac" means to spend a night out, usually on the technical part of the climb. Planned bivouacs are made by expert climbers on long difficult routes that take more than one day; for these, special equipment is carried, such as down clothing, extra water, and (on vertical cliffs) hammocks to sleep in. This type of route is beyond the scope of advanced beginners and intermediate climbers. Bivouacking as described here means spending the night out on snow or rock without planning to.

Preparation

Climbers should always have equipment in their packs for emergencies: dry socks, mittens, a stocking cap, an extra sweater or wool shirt, extra food and bivouac sack. Two plastic trash sacks, long enough to overlap a few inches, afford lightweight and compact protection. A small hole should be cut in the sack which is over your head (so you can breathe). An ensolite square to sit on can literally save your life on snow. It should be at least twenty inches square and three-eighths inch thick. Bivouacking in a storm is a serious matter, and should be assiduously avoided. If caught out, put on *all* your clothing *before* you get chilled.

Choosing a Bivouac Spot

Unless you are racing darkness and it is nip and tuck whether you can get off the difficult climbing by dark, you should pick out a safe and passably comfortable place before the last minute.

On snow, find bare rocks to sit on if you can. If it is windy, get some sort of shelter; a hole dug in the snow helps and sometimes a shallow crevasse can be found. Use your equipment for insulation. You can sit on the rope. Take special care of your feet; the toes are usually the first thing to freeze. Remove your crampons, as they conduct heat away from your feet. Socks worn all day are damp from perspiration if from nothing else; now is the moment for the dry socks you have carried on so many trips. Wiggle your toes frequently. Feet can be put in the rucksack for insulation, or you and your friends can take turns warming each other's feet under clothing.

On rock, look for a ledge large enough so you can move around, or at least so you can sit or even lie down. If the ledge is sloping or skimpy, anchor yourselves and all your equipment; and periodically during the night check the knots. Huddle together for mutual warmth. Take turns in the middle unless one person particularly needs that extra bit of warmth. It is strange but true that you probably will sleep part of the time. It will be a long cold night—but also rather a wonderful night, with a view you will never see again under similar circumstances (or so you hope). Your mutual sufferings will even be hilarious in retrospect.

Resuming Descent

In the morning, allow for the fact that you are pretty well petrified from the cold and the cramped position. Do not start right down as soon as you can see. Move around if it is safe; stretch, eat a little, and try to warm up. Descend with extreme caution until you are off the exposed part of the route. Usually you feel none the worse for wear.

As you pack out, you will turn to look with satisfaction and pleasure at the peak, which already seems far away. You will trace the route with your eyes, and relive the adventure in mind and muscle. Knowing you reached that unattainable-looking summit is a private glory beyond price.

8

Tips on Where to Climb, at Home and Abroad

A CLIMBER may well simply pick out the cliff, aiguille, peak, or boulder of his desire and attempt to climb it. At times, however, he needs some special information. If there is no one to ask, how can he tell if an unknown route matches his abilities? What restrictions on climbing exist in an area? What are some of the conditions to expect and prepare for in a foreign country? These problems are discussed in this chapter.

CLIMBING CLASSIFICATIONS

As soon as your climbing career begins, you will hear routes esoterically described by classes, grades, letters, numbers, and decimal points. These are symbols used in various climbing classification systems to indicate briefly the length, difficulty, and equipment needs on a given climb, and to provide a basis for comparison between climbs. All such rating systems presuppose that you are a competent climber. American rating systems refer to routes that are primarily on rock.

Reasons for Classifying Climbs

Ratings help you choose climbs suitable for your ability, experience, or mood. They furnish a standard of difficulty for use in guidebooks and in climbers' shoptalk, and add interest when you are reading about ascents. They provide approximate criteria for judging the development of your technical skill and how it compares with that of others. The grading systems were not devised as a basis of competition among climbers, but sometimes are used as if they had been.

What Classifications Do Not Do

Ratings are based on good conditions, and on individual climbers' opinions. Every climb differs from all others. Some types of climbing suit individual talents better than others. (You may waltz up slabs but balk in chimneys.) Use the ratings only as a rough guide to difficulty and equipment needs. Do not expect perfect accuracy and uniformity. Use your own judgment always.

How to Understand Rating Systems

First find out what system is used in your local area. Ask climbers and refer to guidebooks. Familiarize yourself with the symbols used to describe climbs you have done, and what they mean in terms of climbing difficulty. Compare a familiar system with the one used in a new area.

Why Several Systems?

Numerous classification systems have existed (and still do) in various climbing centers, both here and abroad. Where a system is firmly established, its proponents understand it perfectly and are reluctant to adopt a new one. However, various rating systems have expanded or changed over the years because of new techniques, and some have been replaced with more widely used systems. There is a trend toward uniformity due to the growing number of climbers that travel from one area to another. Though some of the less well-known systems are still in use and an oc-

casional new one crops up, there are two major climbing classification systems used (either separately or side by side) in most
of the United States and Canada. Whether one or the other will
eventually prevail, or a crossbreed system develop, remains to
be seen.

Major Classification Systems

Two major systems in use at present in the United States and
Canada are the Decimal System (also called the Yosemite Decimal
System or YDS) and the National Climbing Classification System
(NCCS). Like other systems, they change from time to time as
the sport of climbing changes.

Decimal System. This system began with the old Sierra Club
System, which had the original purpose of indicating equipment
needs. The class number describes the most difficult pitch of the
climb. Beginning and intermediate climbers will be primarily con-
cerned with Class 4 and the easier subdivisions of Class 5. As
this basic system is still in use, the original classes are listed.
Later modifications in Classes 5 and 6 are described thereafter,
and it can be seen how classification systems developed to keep
pace with the sport.

Class 1.   Hiking. Any footgear adequate.
Class 2.   Proper footgear necessary for rough terrain. Occa-
           sional handholds used.
Class 3.   Scrambling. Hands may be used frequently. Ropes
           should be available for occasional use.
Class 4.   Ropes and belays must be used continuously for
           safety. Belay anchors may be necessary.
Class 5.   Leader protection required above the belayer.
Class 6.   Direct aid must be used.

As increasingly difficult rock climbing came into vogue with
improved equipment, a majority of climbs fell within Class 5, but
varied greatly in difficulty. Decimals came into use for subdividing
Class 5 climbs by difficulty. Thus Classes 5.0 and 5.1 refer to
easy routes requiring minimal leader protection; Classes 5.8, 5.9,
and 5.10 refer to exceptionally difficult routes, or routes with at

least one very difficult pitch. The standard of difficult rock climbing has become so high in the last few years that the Decimal System has been expanded to include ratings of 5.11 through 5.13, with 5.10 and higher subdivided "a" through "d."

Similar distinctions were originally applied to Class 6 (direct aid) pitches, but Class 6 was dropped in favor of a special Aid rating, indicated by the letter "A"; Aid climbs are divided into five categories of increasing difficulty: A1, A2, A3, A4, and A5. Most Aid climbs require a high degree of skill and technical ability. A new Aid designation is "C" for Clean, indicating that an Aid climb was done hammerless, chocks being placed for aid. Numbers are added to indicate difficulty; for instance, C3 without a hammer is said to approximate the difficulty of A3 done with hammer and pitons.

The class rating describes only the most difficult pitch of a route, which is only one factor in the problems involved in a climb as a whole. Hence the Decimal System adds grades in Roman numerals I through VI to indicate the overall difficulty of the technical part of the climb, and to provide an approximation of the time involved. Following are the times assigned to the grades:

Grade   I.   A few hours
Grade   II.   Half a day
Grade   III.   Most of a day
Grade   IV.   A long day
Grade   V.   A day and a half to two days
Grade   VI.   Several days

The precise implications of the grade ratings vary somewhat from area to area, as climbing conditions vary. They are not used at all where the time element is unimportant. Similarly, decimal and letter designations are not always applicable.

National Climbing Classification System (NCCS). This system resembles the Decimal System in a similar use of six grades based on the length and overall difficulty of a climb, as well as the A1 to A5 categories.

The NCCS describes "difficulty" only by giving examples of climbs in major climbing areas that fall within its categories. Conversion to the system is not easy for a climber from an area for which examples are not given. The NCCS makes no recommendations as to equipment, on the basis that such a choice varies according to each climber's concept of safety requirements. The main difference in its symbols is the use of a different numerical rating for free (non-aid) climbing, with the letter "F" standing for Free. This is the key to which system is being used. Comparable degrees of difficulty are:

NCCS Ratings	Decimal System Ratings
F1	Class 1–2
F2	Class 3
F3	Class 4
F4	Class 5.0–5.2
F5	Class 5.3–5.4
F6	Class 5.5–5.6
F7 through F10	Class 5.7 through 5.10

As to clearly understanding the two systems, there is little room for a serious mix-up at the very bottom of the scale or in the top half. But the range from Decimal Class 3 to Class 5.2, as compared with NCCS F2 to F4, might well be confusing. Since this is the range that applies to the beginning and intermediate climber who may not be able to size up a route by looking at it, some extra attention may be profitably given to these particular ratings.

The theoretical ascent described in Chapter 7 could be Decimal Grade III, with pitches of Class 3, 4, and 5.1 difficulty; or NCCS Grade III with F2, F3, and F4 pitches. The rating that might appear in a guidebook using both systems would be "III, 5.1, F4."

Whatever system you use, let your observations, experience, and enjoyment be the deciding factors in choosing and making a climb.

International and Foreign Systems. There are also several standard classification systems used in foreign countries, which will not immediately affect the American neophyte. These are explained in guidebooks to foreign climbing areas. They are usually not keyed in to the systems used in the United States and Canada, but are correlated with the British system when the books' publishers are English. The traditional British system employs adjectives; a new numerical system has been developed also. The

UIAA *(Union Internationale des Associations d'Alpinisme),* which includes the American Alpine Club as well as organizations in Japan, Europe, and elsewhere, has developed an international rating system. This system has not come into use in American climbing. It uses Grades I through VI, but these "grades" are *not* the same grades in use in the Decimal System and the NCCS. Plus and minus marks are added to the numerals, which indicate shades of ease and difficulty. Further, A1 to A4 describes artificial aid climbing in the UIAA system, and the letter "e" denotes the use of expansion bolts (for instance, A4e). Various guidebooks add local and linguistic variations (e.g., *très difficile*) that are clearly explained.

The correlation of the UIAA system, the British system, and the American systems is useful to help understand the difficulty of climbs one reads about; and will have practical application when (as is likely) climbing is done abroad. The UIAA grades I and II correspond to Decimal classes 1–3, NCCS F1 and F2, and the British Easy and Moderate. Correlations for technical ratings are as follows (gaps represent overlap or imperfect correlation):

Decimal	NCCS	UIAA	British
4	F3	III –	Moderately difficult
5.0	F4	III	
5.1	F4	III +	Difficult
5.2	F4	IV –	Very difficult
5.3	F5	IV	Severe
5.4	F5	IV +	
5.5	F6	V –	
5.6	F6	V	Very severe
5.7	F7	V +	
5.8	F8	VI –	Hard, very severe
5.9	F9	VI	
5.10	F10	VI +	Extreme

CLIMBING REGULATIONS

In some areas permission to climb must be obtained, depending at times on the party's experience. In many places, official permits are required for camping, hiking, or even entering.

Private Property

If you want to climb on private property, or in areas reached by crossing private property, seek the owner's permission. Be courteous, explain your activities, and obey any requests he may have. Do not damage anything on the property, and carry out all your litter.

Indian Reservations

Peaks and pinnacles often have a serious religious significance to the Indian tribes, and should not be ascended without specific permission.

National Parks and Monuments

Many national parks and monuments regulate camping, motor vehicle use, and sometimes climbing. Climbers generally accept the advisability of registering before and after climbs, but it is a moot point among them whether other restrictions are justifiable or effective. Regulations change frequently, and anyone planning to camp and climb in national parks and monuments should find out in advance about current regulations, and check with rangers on arrival. They can often provide useful information about routes and approaches, and may offer suggestions for your safety. Signing out for climbs and signing back in are routine. If any further rules exist, they should be obeyed. Telephone directory listing for national parks will be found under United States Government, Interior, Department of.

Wilderness Areas

Most, if not all, Wilderness Areas and many national forests require permits before climbers and others may enter specific regions. Rules vary from place to place, and from time to time. Possible restrictions may cover the total number of users at any one time, seasonal entry, wildlife refuges, motor vehicles, camping, and open fires. Before making final arrangements to climb in a specific area, apply for a written permit and a list of current regulations from the nearest United States Forest Service office or ranger station, listed in the phone book under United States Government, Agriculture, Department of. The purpose of these restrictions is to preserve the backcountry from destruction or serious damage from overuse or improper use.

CLIMBING IN FOREIGN COUNTRIES

After gaining experience close to home, you may have the opportunity and urge to climb in foreign ranges, where climate, rock, customs and sources of information naturally vary. A bar to collecting information abroad is often language differences, though climbers everywhere usually try to help each other. As much data as possible about areas mentioned here, and others such as the Andes, Himalayas, etc., are best gathered from local climbers who have been there. Your first foreign climbs are most apt to be in either North America or Europe, and a few pointers may help.

Canada

Striking ranges, impressive for beauty, variety, and extensive glaciers, run northerly-southerly in the provinces of British Columbia and Alberta and in the Yukon territory. Many well-known peaks lie within the boundaries of Banff, Jasper, and Glacier national parks, but these comprise only a sampling of the whole array.

Type of Climbing and Weather. The mountains catch heavy precipitation, although the intervening valleys may be quite dry. In some places, glacier climbing is accessible from the highway or by trail. In other areas, peaks are reached by very long strenuous backpacks, up river valleys and through down timber. Rock varies from the shattered limestone of much of the Canadian Rockies to the sound granite of peaks protruding from the glaciers of the Bugaboos in the Purcell Range. Climbers should carry rainproof tents or shelters; a few huts exist, and there are shelters in highway campgrounds in the parks. The weather is most apt to be favorable in July and August, but expect rain and snow at any time.

Sources of Information. Several guidebooks describe climbing in western Canada. They are available through shops for mountaineers or by mail order. Some recent ones are:

A Climber's Guide to the Rocky Mountains of Canada—North, by William L. Putnam, Chris Jones, and Robert Kruszyna. The American Alpine Club and The Alpine Club of Canada, New York, N. Y. 1974.

A Climber's Guide to the Rocky Mountains of Canada—South, by Glen W. Boles with Robert Kruszyna and William L. Putnam. The American Alpine Club and The Alpine Club of Canada, New York, N. Y. 7th ed., 1979.

The Interior Ranges of British Columbia—North, by William L. Putnam. The American Alpine Club, New York, N. Y. 6th ed., 1975.

The Interior Ranges of British Columbia—South, by William L. Putnam and Robert Kruszyna. The American Alpine Club, New York, N. Y. 6th ed., 1977.

Squamish Chief Guide, by Gordon Smaill. Bill Lupul and Marlene Smaill, Vancouver, British Columbia. 1975.

Topographical maps can be obtained at national park headquarters or by writing to the Map Distribution Office, Department of Mines and Technical Surveys, Ottawa, Ontario. Information not otherwise available may be obtained through the Alpine Club of Canada, Box 1026, Banff, Alberta. The ACC also publishes the *Canadian Alpine Journal* annually.

Climbing Regulations. There are few, if any, restrictions on climbing in Canada, but there are some as to where you may make high camps in the parks. Check your plans with a park warden (the counterpart of a ranger). One "must" is to sign out for contemplated climbs, and sign back in promptly on your return.

Border Regulations. Crossing the border into Canada presents few problems. No passport or other identification is required, but there are a few restrictions on what may be taken in. Obtain a special insurance card covering automobile travel in Canada from your agent.

Mexico

Climbers are primarily interested in two areas in Mexico: the mountainous regions in Baja (Lower) California, and the high glaciated volcanic peaks near Mexico City.

Baja California. The landscape is similar to that of Southern California, with desert at low elevations and coniferous forests above. The highest peak in the region is called Picacho del Diablo by climbers, and Cerro de la Encantada on maps. It is 10,125 feet high, and is reached by a long backpack up a spectacular gorge, and an obscure climbing route. This area is covered in: *Camping and Climbing in Baja,* by John W. Robinson, La Siesta Press, Glendale, Calif. 1972.

The Glacier Peaks. The three highest peaks (among countless others) are Popocatépetl (Popo), 17,761 feet high; Ixtaccihuatl (Ixta), 17,343 feet high; and Citlaltépetl (Orizaba), 18,851 feet high, the highest point in Mexico. The regular routes are glacier climbs of moderate difficulty. The high elevations add to the exertion. Crampons, ice axes, and snow goggles are required; a rope should be carried. The best climbing season is from mid-November through February–the dry season. Climbers from the United States find the Thanksgiving and Christmas holidays admirably synchronized with the Mexican climbing season. Huts serve most of the routes. Take your own stove.

Sources of Information. Details of climbing the Mexican volcanoes are described in *Mexico's Volcanoes: A Climber's Guide,* by R.J.Secor. The Mountaineers, Seattle, Wash. 1981. For additional information contact Club de Exploraciónes de México, Apartado Postal 10134, México 8, D.F., México.

Health Problems. Tourists in Mexico, as elsewhere, sometimes fall victim to a digestive disorder (known among climbers as Montezuma's Revenge). It is not serious, and of course not everyone gets it; but it could spoil your climbing plans. As a preventive, eat only the food you have along until you are through climbing; take your own water, drink bottled water, or use water-purifying tablets (chlorine or iodine types) available at drugstores. As in many places, keep track of your belongings.

Border Regulations. A tourist card, required for more than a brief stay, may be obtained at a Mexican consulate or a Department of Tourism office, or at the border. Proof of United States citizenship is required. Persons under twenty-one must have a letter of permission from parents or guardian. If driving, ask your insurance agent about special requirements; the usual procedure is to buy Mexican coverage at a United States border town. Buses go almost everywhere in Mexico.

Europe

Climbing is a popular and respected pursuit in Europe. (You won't wonder why when you see the Alps.) You will find that several aspects of European mountaineering are quite different from climbing in the United States.

Huts. Backpacking and high camps, an integral part of American climbing, exist only on a small scale in Europe. There are hundreds of well-supplied accommodations, conveniently located as starting points for almost every climb. They exist primarily or solely for the comfort and safety of climbers. Most of these huts are built and managed by the large Alpine clubs, and some by government agencies. A long hike or climb is often necessary to reach the huts, but once you are there, you are supplied with shelter, blankets, sometimes pillows, and usually any meals you wish. There is no need to carry a sleeping bag, and no use for a packframe. A rucksack easily holds all your needs: climbing equipment, clothing, and personal belongings. The huts and refuges range from small ones for seldom climbed routes, or emergency shelters, to large hotels. Accommodations may be dormitories or "mattress rooms," bunk rooms for four to six people, or even private rooms with sheets on the beds. The more modest accommodations cost very little. Most of the huts are staffed in the climbing season with one or more persons, who cook, serve, clean, keep order, and wake climbers before dawn.

Food and Water at Huts. You can take all or part of your food, cook it yourself or sometimes have it cooked for you; or order all your meals at many of the huts. An economical and satisfactory system is to purchase rucksack foods at the towns below—bread, butter, cheese, sausage, sugar, tea bags, etc., for breakfast and lunch; and order soups, beverages, and dinners at the huts. Prices vary depending on where and what you eat, but are relatively low. All sorts of beverages, including wines, are available except the plain cold water that Americans are used to. Order hot water by the liter for tea or coffee; the insignificant cost includes cups. What water supplies there are sometimes seem dubious; it is usually best to drink only boiled or bottled water, or add purifying tablets. Take a water bottle.

Clothing and Miscellany Needed. Most European climbers appear better dressed than bushwhacking, camping Americans. Expect cold wet weather, even during July and August, the best months. A plastic raincoat or poncho is essential. For some huts you need slippers or extra shoes, as climbing boots are forbidden for indoor wear. You should provide spare trousers, in case yours get wet; the huts are usually unheated in summer, and wet clothing dries slowly. A small foreign-language dictionary may be indispensable, and reading and writing materials are useful for stormy days.

Gathering Information. Some of the things you need to know are best looked into before leaving home, others at the European climbing centers. Climbers' guidebooks in French or German are prolific in Europe, but to be sure of having an English edition buy them in America or England.

When you arrive in a European town near your selected climb, go to the tourist or information bureau, or climbing club office, to inquire about local huts. The "approach" to the hut may combine a trip by car, funicular, and cog railway, and walking or climbing. Railways serve many areas not reached by roads. Topographical maps that show roads, railways, funiculars, trails, huts, peaks, and elevations (in meters) can be purchased at tourist bureaus or book stores. If you have no one to climb with, or are inexperienced, guides can be hired at climbing centers and will take care of all arrangements. Of course, European climbers are glad to help you if you can break the language barrier. By no means do all Europeans speak English; those who do often reach a point where they can go no further—your own situation exactly, with languages learned in school. Don't hesitate to try a few foreign words—it pleases people. After that, speak English slowly, repeat as necessary, avoid idioms, and try synonyms. At least, everyone has a laugh.

On good climbing days, popular routes on well-known peaks

are usually easy to find. They are apt to be quite crowded with guided and amateur parties of several nationalities.

Climbing Equipment. Whether to take your own clothing and equipment, or to rent or buy it abroad, poses a problem. It depends on the state of your own equipment, your travel weight allowance, and your finances. You will want to buy at least some outing equipment in Europe. The mountaineering shops are prolific. Climbing footgear is sold also in many shoe stores. Before leaving the United States, find out whether there is any duty on clothing and equipment bought in Europe (used or unused while you are abroad). And remember that much equipment sold in the United States has been imported, and might preferably be selected in Europe and if necessary shipped home by mail or freight.

Foreign Climbing Clubs. There are far too many climbing and outing clubs abroad to list them all. Membership in a European Alpine club entitles you to greatly reduced rates for food and lodging at most of the huts, and is worthwhile for a long stay. Some major Alpine clubs are:

Austria. Österreichischer Alpenverein, Wilhelm Greilstrasse 15, 6010 Innsbruck, Austria.

France. Club Alpin Français, Paris-Chamonix Section, 7, Rue la Boétie, Paris 8e, France. Offices in Chamonix open during the summer.

Germany. Deutscher Alpenverein. Praterinsel 5, München 22, Germany.

Great Britain. The Alpine Club, 74 S. Audley St., London, W1, England; Fell and Rock Climbing Club of the English Lake District, Cheshire, England; Association of Scottish Climbing Clubs, 406 Sauchiehall, Glascow C2, Scotland.

Italy. Club Alpino Italiano, Torino, Italy.

Switzerland. Schweizer Alpenclub, Helvetia Platz 4, 3005 Bern, Switzerland.

Mountaineering clubs, climbing guidebooks, and other sources of information for the United States will be listed in the next chapter.

9

Sources of Information
for Climbers

IT IS not hard to collect information about climbing when you know where to find it. Other climbers are, of course, a major source of information. Whenever they get together they like to talk about ascents, discuss techniques, argue about equipment, and regale one another with anecdotes. They gather at meetings, parties, and on the rocks. They write prolifically about their sport, and in other ways find the exchange of climbing information part of their life. A few suggestions about these sources of information and others will give you a good start in finding out the many things you want to know.

CLUBS

Clubs for climbers and mountaineers abound in the United States and elsewhere. General outdoor or conservation clubs often have specialized climbing sections, and a few large associations include several or many scattered climbing groups. Most colleges and universities, and some high schools, have outing or climbing clubs.

Most such organizations offer formal or informal instruction. Appreciate the fact that club members operate strictly as volunteers. Charges, if any, usually cover out-of-pocket expenses. Clubs also present programs about climbing (lectures, slides, and movies), and publish a wide variety of news sheets, bulletins, annual journals, guidebooks, and other informative material. A list follows of some of the larger clubs that can provide much information about various regions, often including names of climbing groups in specific areas.

Adirondack Mountain Club, Inc., 172 Ridge St., Glens Falls, New York.

American Alpine Club, 113 E. 90th St., New York, New York (no outings).

Appalachian Mountain Club, 5 Joy St., Boston, Massachusetts.

Chicago Mountaineering Club, 2901 S. Parkway, Chicago, Illinois.

Colorado Mountain Club, 2530 W. Alameda Ave., Denver, Colorado.

Iowa Mountaineers, P. O. Box 163, Iowa City, Iowa.

Mazamas, 909 N.W. Nineteenth Ave., Portland, Oregon.

The Mountaineers, 719 Pike St., Seattle, Washington.

New England Trail Conference, Box 241, Princeton, Massachusetts.

Potomac Appalachian Trail Club, 1718 N St., N.W., Washington, D.C.

Sierra Club, 530 Bush St., San Francisco, California (nationwide).

Wasatch Mountain Club, 425 S. 8th W., Salt Lake City, Utah.

MOUNTAINEERING SHOPS

Stores that carry mountaineering equipment (often in conjunction with skiing, backpacking, and general sporting goods) may have climbers on the staff, and are usually in touch with the local climbing scene. They often can provide information and advice about equipment, guidebooks for local areas, and qualified climbing schools. Visits to one or several mountain shops are well worthwhile. Such shops are listed in the classified telephone directory under such headings as Mountain Climbing Equipment and Sporting Goods.

Some mountaineering shops publish helpful and informative

catalogs (some free, some available for a fee). Mail order is often a great convenience, especially for climbers who don't live near retail outlets. Some of the concerns that issue catalogs have branch stores in several locations. A few of the available catalogs are listed below.

Campmor, P.O. Box 999-CC, Paramus, New Jersey 07662.

Chouinard Equipment, P.O. Box 90, Department NM, Ventura, California 93002.

Early Winters, 110 Prefontaine Pl. S., Seattle, Washington 98104.

Eastern Mountain Sports, Inc., Vose Farm Rd., Peterborough, New Hampshire 03458.

Forrest Mountaineering, 1517 Platte St., Denver, Colorado 80202.

The Gendarme, P.O. Box 53, Seneca Rocks, West Virginia 26884.

Holubar Mountaineering, Ltd., 1975 30th St., Boulder, Colorado 80302.

Indiana Camp Supply, Inc., P.O. Box 344, Pittsboro, Indiana 46167.

International Mountain Equipment, Inc., P.O. Box 494, Main St., North Conway, New Hampshire 03860.

Mountain High, Ltd., 824 Graaf, Ridgecrest, California 93555.

Mountain Safety Research, P.O. Box 3978, Terminal Station, Seattle, Washington 98124.

Recreational Equipment, Inc., 1525 11th Ave., Seattle, Washington 98122.

Sierra Designs, P.O. Box 12930, Oakland, California 94604.

The Ski Hut, P.O. Box 309, Berkeley, California 94701.

BOOKS, JOURNALS, AND PERIODICALS

A large body of fine mountaineering literature deals with classical and recent ascents, expeditions, biography, and mountain philosophies the world over. These engrossing books are found in club and public libraries, some bookstores, and many mountaineering shops. They are not named here; you will discover them for yourself and reap countless hours of pleasure from them.

Publications of practical and current interest in the climbing world include instructional material, regional guidebooks, and maps. Mountaineering magazines and annual journals of climbing clubs keep readers up-to-date on techniques, controversial viewpoints, and ascents. The lists below suggest the scope of material available, but are far from all-inclusive. Local mountaineering outlets or the offices of large clubs are good places to find these publications and others, especially guidebooks of local climbing areas. Representative publications in each category are listed, but this is only a sampling of the whole array.

Books of Mountaineering Instruction

Advanced Rockcraft, by Royal Robbins. La Siesta Press, Glendale, CA. 1973.

Basic Rockcraft, by Royal Robbins, La Siesta Press, Glendale, CA. 1971.

Climbing Ice, by Yvon Chouinard. Sierra Club Books in association with the American Alpine Club. San Francisco, CA. 1978.

Icecraft, by Norman Kingsley. La Siesta Press, Glendale, CA. 1975.

The Ice Experience, by Jeff Lowe. Contemporary Books, Inc., Chicago, IL. 1979.

Learning to Rock Climb, by Michael Loughman. Sierra Club Books, San Francisco, CA. 1981.

Mountaineering: The Freedom of the Hills, Ed Peters, ed. The Mountaineers, Seattle, WA. 4th ed., 1982.

Books on Mountain Emergencies

The ABC of Avalanche Safety, by Edward R. LaChapelle. The Mountaineers, Seattle, WA. 1978.

Going High: The Story of Man and Altitude, by Charles S. Houston, M.D. The American Alpine Club, New York, NY. 1980.

Hypothermia and Frostbite, by James A. Wilkerson, M.D. The Mountaineers, Seattle, WA. 1982.

Medicine for Mountaineering, by James A. Wilkerson, M.D. The Mountaineers, Seattle,WA. 2nd ed., 1975.

Mountain Sickness: Prevention, Recognition and Treatment,

by Peter Hackett, M.D. The American Alpine Club, New York, NY. 1980.

Wilderness Search and Rescue, by Tim J. Setnicka. Appalachian Mountain Club, Boston, MA. 1980.

Books on Approach and Camping

Backcountry Basics, by Bradford Angier. Stackpole Books, Harrisburg, PA. 1983.

Backpack Cookery, by Ruth Dyar Mendenhall. La Siesta Press, Glendale, CA. Revised ed., 1974.

Backpack Techniques, by Ruth Dyar Mendenhall. La Siesta Press, Glendale, CA. Revised ed., 1973.

Gorp, Glop & Glue Stew, by Yvonne Prater and Ruth Dyar Mendenhall. The Mountaineers, Seattle, WA. 1982.

Club Publications

Accidents in North American Mountaineering. Annual report of the Safety Committees of American Alpine Club, New York, NY and Alpine Club of Canada, Banff, Alberta.

American Alpine Journal. Annual. American Alpine Club, New York, NY.

Magazines

Climbing. Aspen, CO. Bimonthly.

Summit, A Mountaineering Magazine. Big Bear Lake, CA. Bimonthly.

Climbers' Guidebooks

Cascade Alpine Guide, Climbing and High Routes: Columbia River to Stevens Pass, by Fred Beckey. The Mountaineers, Seattle, WA. 1973.

Cascade Alpine Guide, Climbing and High Routes: Rainy Pass to Fraser River, by Fred Beckey. The Mountaineers, Seattle, WA. 1981.

Cascade Alpine Guide, Climbing and High Routes: Stevens Pass to Rainy Pass, by Fred Beckey. The Mountaineers, Seattle, WA. 1977.

A Climber's Guide to Devil's Lake, by William Widula and Steve Olaf Swartling. University of Wisconsin Press, Madison, WI. 1979.

A Climber's Guide to the Olympic Mountains, by Olympic Mountain Rescue. The Mountaineers, Seattle, WA. Second ed., 1979.

A Climbing Guide to Oregon, by Nicholas A. Dodge, Touchstone Press, Beaverton, OR. 1975.

A Climber's Guide to Tahquitz and Suicide Rocks, by Chuck Wilts. American Alpine Club, New York, NY. 6th ed., 1979.

A Climber's Guide to the Teton Range, by Leigh Ortenburger. Sierra Club Books, San Francisco, CA. Condensed ed., 1973.

Climbing and Hiking in the Wind River Mountains, by Joe Kelsey. Sierra Club Books, San Francisco, CA. 1980.

Guide to the Colorado Mountains, by Robert Ormes. Colorado Mountain Club, Colorado Springs, CO. 1979.

Rocky Heights, A Guide to Boulder Free Climbs, by James S. Erikson. J.S.E., Boulder, CO. 1980.

Shawangunk Rock Climbs, by Richard C. Williams. American Alpine Club, New York, NY. 1980.

Southern Rock, A Climber's Guide, by Chris Hall. East Wood Press Books, Charlotte, NC. 1981.

Stony Point Guide, by Paul Hellweg and Donald B. Fisher. La Siesta Press, Glendale, CA. 1982.

Traprock–Rock Climbing in Central Connecticut, by Ken Nichols. American Alpine Club, New York, NY. 1982.

Washington Rock: A Climber's Guide, by Don Brooks. The Mountaineers, Seattle, WA. 1982.

MAPS

Pertinent maps for an area are usually included in guidebooks. Most such maps should be augmented by topographical maps of the United States Geodetic Survey. These can be purchased in map stores or mountaineering shops, or ordered by mail from the Distribution Center, United States Geological Survey, Federal

Center, Denver, Colorado 80225, or Washington Map Distribution Center, United States Geological Survey, 1200 Eads St., Arlington, Virginia 22202. Various Forest Service and National Park headquarters can often provide large-scale topographical maps or special trail maps helpful in a specific area.

COMMERCIAL CLIMBING SERVICES

Climbing schools and guide services can be found in many national parks, and in or near other vacation and climbing locations. They are helpful for a beginner who has no other way to learn, or who just wants to "try it out." However, the serious beginner, who wants to continue technical climbing, must find more permanent companions when the usually brief formal instruction on rock or snow has come to an end.

Various travel services also conduct trips devoted to or slanted toward mountaineering.

Mountaineering shops or club members may be able to recommend qualified services. Addresses can be located in advertisements in some mountaineering publications. Such services are also sometimes listed in classified telephone directories under such headings as Mountain Climbing Instruction. Send for brochures and information; ask about dates, what equipment you must furnish, fees, etc. And try to determine whether those in charge are experienced and well qualified in their fields.

FINIS

All these sources of information are good ones, and some are fundamental to competence and safety. But in the end, you will learn the most from the mountains themselves. Enjoy them; treat them with respect. In turn, the peaks teach you the wonders of being alone with yourself and creation.

Index

Page numbers in italics refer to illustrations.